ESSENTIAL FLORENCE AND TUSCANY

Original text by Tim Jepson
Updated by Lindsay Bennett

© AA Media Limited 2010
First published 2008
Information verified and updated 2010. Reprinted February 2011.

ISBN: 978-0-7495-6527-5

Published by AA Publishing, a trading name of AA Media Limited, whose registered office is Fanum House, Basing View, Basingstoke, Hampshire RG21 4EA.
Registered number 06112600.

Colour separation: MRM Graphics Ltd. Printed and bound in Italy by Printer Trento S.r.l.

Find out more about AA Publishing and the wide range of services the AA provides by visiting our website at theAA.com/shop

A04628
Maps in this title produced from mapping © MAIRDUMONT/Falk Verlag 2011
Transport map © Communicarta Ltd, UK

About this book

This book is divided into five sections.

The essence of Florence and Tuscany pages 6–19

Introduction; Features; Food and drink; Short break, including the 10 Essentials

Planning pages 20–33

Before you go; Getting there; Getting around; Being there

Best places to see pages 34–55

The unmissable highlights

Best things to do pages 56–73

Good places to have lunch; Stunning views; Great shopping in Florence; Best Tuscan hill towns and more

Exploring pages 74–185

The best places to visit in Florence and Tuscany, organized by area

Maps

All map references are to the maps on the covers. For example, the Ponte Vecchio has the reference ✚ *Firenze 4e* – indicating the grid square in which it is to be found

Admission prices

Inexpensive (under €3)
Moderate (€3–€6)
Expensive (over €6)

Hotel prices

Prices are per room per night: € budget (under €140); €€ moderate (€140–€220); €€€ expensive (over €220)

Restaurant prices

Price for a three-course meal per person without drinks: € budget (under €30); €€ moderate (€30–€50); €€€ expensive (over €50)

Contents

BEST THINGS TO DO

EXPLORING...

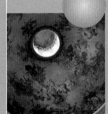

The essence of...

Florence (Firenze) seduces with its art and culture, Tuscany with its hill towns and timeless scenery. Europe's greatest Renaissance paintings and sculptures crowd the city's churches and galleries, while ancient vineyards, gnarled olives and cypress-topped hills make up one of Italy's most beautiful regional landscapes. Beyond the lures of culture and countryside, however, lie more subtle charms: the simple pleasures of a hazy-hilled view, for example; or the best ice creams and tastiest cappuccinos in Europe; bustling bars and open-air cafés; dining under the stars; or a stroll around geranium-hung streets on a summer evening.

features

Florence is not entirely devoted to art, and visitors who restrict themselves to paintings and sculpture will come away with memories of a forbidding indoor city. It's essential to leave the rather gloomy streets and brooding palaces for the city's gardens, bridges and half-hidden corners, and still more vital to join the Florentines – some of the most chic of all Italians – in their pursuit of outdoor pleasures, whether it's window shopping in Via dei Tornabuoni or sipping drinks in the city's elegant, old-world cafés.

In Tuscany the choice of pleasure is greater still, from cities with a wide array of culture – notably Siena and Lucca – to the endless possibilities of the region's beautiful countryside. There are hills, mountains, sandy beaches, and a hundred village squares lined with rustic trattorias and bustling bars. And not so far from the beaten track lie towns such as Pienza, Cortona and San Gimignano, each a perfect combination of the culture, charm and beauty that make this unusually blessed region so irresistible.

GEOGRAPHY
- Latitude of Florence: 43° 46 minutes north – the same latitude as Toronto (Canada) and Sapporo (Japan)
- Longitude of Florence: 11° 14 minutes east
- Area of the Tuscany region: 22,992sq km (8,875sq miles)
- Altitude of Florence: 49m (161ft) above sea level
- Height of Duomo: 85m (280ft)
- Highest point in Tuscany: Mt Cimone, 2,165m (7,101ft)
- Most densely wooded region in Italy: Tuscany
- Length of the River Arno, in Tuscany: 241km (790ft)

CLIMATE
- Average January temperature: 6°C (43°F)
- Average August temperature: 25°C (77°F)
- Average October rainfall: 12.4cm (5in)
- Average July rainfall: 3.5cm (1.5in)
- Average annual rainfall: 89.4cm (35in)
- Height above street level of 1966 flood: 6m (19ft)

PEOPLE
- Population of Florence in May 2009: 369,321
- Population in June 1999: 376,662
- Population in June 1996: 380,058
- Population of Tuscany: 3.5 million

TOURISM
- Annual number of visitors to Florence: 7 million (estimate)
- Most popular museum and gallery: Uffizi
- Annual number of visitors to the Uffizi: about 1.5 million

THE ESSENCE OF FLORENCE AND TUSCANY

food & drink

Poverty and peasant traditions have long inspired Tuscan cooking, with the result that the region's cuisine relies on simple, fresh ingredients and straightforward preparation and presentation. Simplicity is the keynote of most antipasti (starters), which include hams, salamis and crostini (small rounds of toasted bread with mushroom, olive, chicken liver and other pâté-like toppings).

Typical first courses *(primi)* are *pappardelle alla lepre* (noodles in a hare sauce); *pici*, a Sienese pasta; vegetable-based *minestrone*; *pappa al pomodoro*, a tomato and basil soup thickened with bread; *risotto*, often with the region's prized *porcini* mushrooms; and *ribollita*, a soup of beans, cabbage, vegetables and bread. Beans are so ubiquitous in the region's cuisine – notably in *zuppa di fagioli* – that other Italians lampoon the Tuscans as *mangiafagioli* (bean-eaters).

MAIN COURSES

Meat and fish (on the coast) provide the focal point of most main courses *(secondi)*. The best-known dish is the majestic *bistecca alla fiorentina*, a large T-bone steak drizzled with olive oil, seasoned with herbs and grilled over the embers of a chestnut-wood fire. Other grilled meats *(alla griglia)* are also common, especially lamb *(agnello)*, pork *(maiale)* and chicken *(pollo)*. Game and wild boar *(cinghiale)* are often available. A mixed grill is known as *arrosto misto*; a casserole-type sauce of meat, tomatoes and olives is known as *alla cacciatore* ('hunter-style'). Tuscan *scottiglia* is a stew of poultry, white wine and veal *(vitello)*.

DESSERTS

Desserts can disappoint in restaurants, often because they are made off the premises or laced with a virulent liqueur. Most Tuscans prefer fresh fruit *(frutta fresca)* – grapes, strawberries, cherries – or stroll to a *gelateria* for an ice cream. Specialties include: *cantuccini*, almond biscuits dipped in dessert wine, or Siena's famous *panforte*, a tasty combination of nuts and candied fruit. Cheese *(formaggio)* is also a good bet, especially sheep's cheese *(pecorino)*.

WINE

Once upon a time Tuscan wine began and ended with Chianti. These days the region's wines are undergoing a renaissance, with many producers beginning to concentrate on high-quality (and high-priced) wines. The grading system (DOC) is slightly discredited; many producers make wine independently, outside classification, known as *Vino da Tavola* and they are often better than DOC wine. Many are also experimenting with new grape varieties, blending French imports such as Cabernet Sauvignon with local staples such as Sangiovese (the grape used to make Chianti). *Sassicaia*, *Tignanello* and *Carmignano* are the best known of these 'Super Tuscans'.

Chianti is still the region's most famous wine, though two other great names offer more rewarding tipples if you can afford them: Brunello, from the area around Montalcino, is one of Italy's most majestic wines, produced by a bewildering array of tiny vineyards clustered around the ancient hill town. Its younger cousin,

Rosso di Montalcino, is a less expensive but still outstanding alternative. Names to look for include *Carpazo*, *Castello Romitorio* and the reasonably priced *Il Poggione*. Tuscany's other great wine is *Vino Nobile*, the ancient 'king of wines', produced around Montepulciano by estates such as Cantucci, Poliziano and Vecchia Cantina.

Reds have traditionally overshadowed the region's whites, the exceptions being *Galestro*, a light generic wine made by several producers, and *Vernaccia di San Gimignano*, which for years suffered a catastrophic fall in quality and prestige and is now making a comeback. Most

Vernaccia sold in San Gimignano's shops, however, is insipid plonk. If you want quality go for wines from Guicciardini's Cusona estate, makers of *Vernaccia* for 500 years, Teruzzi & Puthod's *Carmen* and *Terra di Tufo*, and Falchini's *Casale* and *Vigna a Solatio*.

short break

If you only have a short time to visit Florence and Tuscany and would like to take home some unforgettable memories, you can do something local and capture the real flavour of the area. The following suggestions will give you a wide range of sights and experiences that won't take long, won't cost very much and will make your visit very special.

● **See Michelangelo's *David*** – so familiar it's a cliché, but something you still have to see (➤ 40–41).

● **Climb the Campanile** – struggle up the stairs for a breathtaking view of Florence (➤ 80–81). Alternatively, climb to the top of the cathedral dome for a similar panorama (➤ 42–43).

● **Sip a drink in the Campo** – treat yourself to a drink in a café on Siena's Piazza del Campo, one of Italy's most beautiful medieval squares (➤ 50–51).

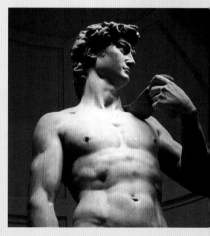

● **Eat an ice cream** – buy an ice cream from Vivoli (► 68), in Florence, widely considered to be one of Italy's best *gelaterie*, and eat it sitting in nearby Piazza Santa Croce.

● **Visit Santa Croce** – Tuscany's greats are buried in this church in Florence, among them Michelangelo, Galileo and Machiavelli. As an added attraction there are frescoes by Giotto and other medieval artists (► 52–53).

● **Take an evening stroll** *(passeggiata)* – head for the Arno bridges, and the Ponte Vecchio in particular, for some of Florence's most romantic night-time views (► 108–109).

- **Walk in the Boboli Gardens** – 5 million visitors a year can't be wrong: take a break from sightseeing in Italy's most visited gardens (➤ 88).

- **Enjoy an al fresco lunch** – eating out is one of Tuscany's greatest pleasures: find a restaurant with outside tables and forget the sightseeing in favour of a leisurely lunch (➤ 58–59).

- **Visit San Gimignano** – busy in summer, but still the village to see in Tuscany if you see no other; known as the 'medieval Manhattan' after its ancient towers (➤ 162).

- **See the top museums** – you can't escape the art: Be sure to visit the Uffizi for the paintings (➤ 44–45) – reserve ahead – and the Bargello for the sculpture (➤ 46–47).

Planning

Before you go

WHEN TO GO

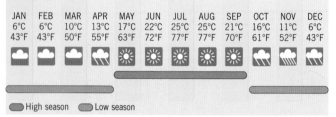

JAN	FEB	MAR	APR	MAY	JUN	JUL	AUG	SEP	OCT	NOV	DEC
6°C	6°C	10°C	13°C	17°C	22°C	25°C	25°C	21°C	16°C	11°C	6°C
43°F	43°F	50°F	55°F	63°F	72°F	77°F	77°F	70°F	61°F	52°F	43°F

High season   Low season

The best times to visit Florence (Firenze) are late March to early June and mid-September to mid-November, when the weather is generally fine but not too hot. Avoid July and August, when the city is not only stifling and uncomfortable, but also extremely crowded. August can also be humid and thunderstorms are possible in summer and through September and October. Winters are short but can be cold, notably in January and February, though these two months are also the quietest periods of the year. Snow is rare. The Tuscan countryside is at its best in spring, from around late March to late May, later in the mountains. Note that Florence is also busy around Easter and major religious holidays or events and during school holidays.

WHAT YOU NEED

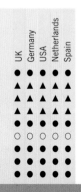

● Required
○ Suggested
▲ Not required

Some countries require a passport to remain valid for a minimum period (usually at least six months) beyond the date of entry – check before you travel.

	UK	Germany	USA	Netherlands	Spain
Passport (or National Identity Card where applicable)	●	●	●	●	●
Visa (regulations can change – check before you travel)	▲	▲	▲	▲	▲
Onward or Return Ticket	▲	▲	▲	▲	▲
Health Inoculations	▲	▲	▲	▲	▲
Health Documentation (► 23, Health Insurance)	●	●	●	●	●
Travel Insurance	○	○	○	○	○
Driving Licence	●	●	●	●	●
Car Insurance Certificate (if own car)	●	●	●	●	●
Car Registration Document (if own car)	●	●	●	●	●

WEBSITES

www.initaly.com
www.italyheaven.co.uk
www.turismo.toscana.it

www.firenze.net
www.comune.firenze.it
www.italiantourism.com

TOURIST OFFICES AT HOME

In the UK

Italian State Tourist Board
1 Princes Street,
London W1R 8AY
☎ 020 7408 1254
www.italiantouristboard.co.uk;
www.enit.it

In the USA

Italian Government Travel Office
(ENIT)
630 Fifth Avenue, Suite 1565,
Rockefeller Center, New York
NY 10111 ☎ 212/245-5618

12400 Wilshire Boulevard, Suite
550, Los Angeles, CA 90025
☎ 310/820-1898

HEALTH INSURANCE

Nationals of EU countries receive medical treatment at reduced cost
and pay a percentage of prescribed medicines. Hospital treatment is at
reduced cost. You need a qualifying document (EHIC – European Health
Insurance Card). Private medical insurance is still advised, and is essential
for all other visitors. Nationals of EU countries can obtain dental treatment
at reduced cost from dentists who operate within the Italian health
service. A qualifying document (EHIC) is needed. Again, private medical
insurance is advised for all.

TIME DIFFERENCES

| GMT | Italy | Germany | USA (NY) | Netherlands | Spain |
| 12 noon | 1PM | 1PM | 7AM | 1PM | 1PM |

Italy is one hour ahead of Greenwich Mean Time (GMT+1), but from late
March, when clocks are put forward one hour, to late September, Italian
Summer Time (GMT+2) operates.

NATIONAL HOLIDAYS

1 Jan *New Year's Day*

6 Jan *Epiphany*

Mar/Apr *Easter Sunday and Monday*

25 Apr *Liberation Day, 1945*

1 May *Labour Day*

2 Jun *Republic Day*

15 Aug *Assumption of the Virgin*

1 Nov *All Saints' Day*

8 Dec *Immaculate Conception*

25 Dec *Christmas Day*

26 Dec *St Stephen's Day*

Banks, businesses and most shops and museums are closed on these days, and the road and rail networks are very busy. Florence celebrates its patron saint (St John the Baptist) on 24 June, but most places stay open.

WHAT'S ON WHEN

January *Pitti Immagine:* Florence fashion shows (www.pittimmagine.com).

February Carnival celebrations across Tuscany, notably processions in Viareggio and San Gimignano (Shrove Tuesday and adjacent weekends).

March *Festa dell'Annunziata:* fair in Florence's Piazza Santissima Annunziata (25th).

April Lucca's summer *Sagra Musicale* (Music Festival) begins.
Holy Week celebrations in many towns and villages.
Mostra dell'Artigianato (Florence): international exhibition of crafts and artisans' work (last week).
Scoppo del Carro

(Explosion of the Cart): Easter Sunday service in Florence's Duomo followed by special fireworks.

May *Festa del Grillo:* crickets are sold and released in Florence's Cascine park (Sun after Ascension).
Maggio Musicale (Florence): international festival of music and dance (www.maggiofiorentino.com).
Pisa's 'Historic Regatta of the Maritime Republics' (May–end June).

June Start of summer arts and music festival in San Gimignano.
Luminaria di San Ranieri: fireworks and illuminated streets in Pisa, followed the next day by a historic regatta.
Calcio in Costume: medieval soccer match in Florence.
Il Gioco del Ponte: Pisa's costumed 'Battle of the Bridge' (last Sunday).
Estate Fiesolana: arts and music festival in Fiesole (www.estatefiesolana.it).

July *Corso del Palio:* world-famous horse race in Siena's main square on 2 July (www.ilpalio.org). A second is held on 16 August.
Festa di San Paolino (Lucca): crossbow contest and procession.
Opera festival at Barga near Lucca (second half).
Settimana Musicale Senese: week-long music festival in Siena (last week).
Festival Pucciniano: outdoor festival of Puccini's music held at Torre del Lago, near Lucca (www.puccinifestival.it), during July and August.

August *Cantiere Internazionale* (Montepulciano): festival of contemporary music and dance (first half of month; www.fondazionecantiere.it).
Montepulciano food festival (second Sunday).
Luminaria di Santa Croce (Lucca): torchlit procession.
Bravio delle Botti: (Montepulciano): barrel-rolling contest (last Sunday).
International festival of choral music in Arezzo (last two weeks).

September *Festa delle Rificolone* (Florence): torchlit procession.
Giostra del Saracino (Arezzo): jousting contest in medieval costume (first Sunday; www.giostradelsaracino.arezzo.it).
Wine festivals across the region, notably Greve.

October Florence opera and classical music season, the Teatro Comunale.

Getting there

BY AIR

Pisa (Galileo Galilei) Airport

2km (1.25 miles) to city centre

🚋 5 minutes

🚌 4 minutes

🚗 10 minutes

Florence Perétola Airport

5km (3 miles) to city centre

🚋 N/A

🚌 10 minutes

🚗 30 minutes

The main entry into Tuscany is Pisa (Galileo Galilei) Airport (☎ 050/849 300; www.pisa-airport.com), though flights serve Perétola, close to Florence (☎ 055/306 1300; www.aeroporto.firenze.it). There is a direct rail link between Florence and Pisa Airport (journey time 1 hour).

BY TRAIN
Two major railway lines serve Tuscany, both of which carry sleeper and other international train services. The first links Florence's main Santa Maria Novella train station to Bologna to the north and Rome to the south. Trains run on this line from France, Switzerland, Germany, Austria and elsewhere. The second runs down the Tuscan coast, connecting Pisa, Livorno and other Tuscan towns and cities to Rome to the south and Genoa and the French Riviera to the north. Visit www.trenitalia.com.

BY CAR
Florence lies close to Italy's main *autostrada* (motorway), the A1, which provides the main approach to the city from Bologna and the north and Rome and the south. On the coast, the A12 provides the main link to Pisa, which is connected in turn to Florence by the A11. Note that tolls are payable on Italian motorways.

BY BUS
Eurolines (0870 514 3219 in the UK, 055/357 059 in Italy; www.eurolines. com) provides long-distance buses to Florence and Siena from the UK and elsewhere, but the services are much slower and often no cheaper than flights or train services. Most long-distance bus services run to the bus station just to the west of the main Santa Maria Novella train station.

BY BOAT
Ferries and cruise ships dock on the Tuscan coast at Livorno, with services to and from Corsica, Sardinia, southern France and elsewhere. Local ferries also link the Tuscan mainland with Elba, Capraia and the other islands of the Tuscan archipelago. Ferries also operate between Porto Santo Stefano and other points on the Argentario peninsula near Orbetello to the islands of Giglio and Giannutri. For more information visit www.traghetti.com.

Getting around

PUBLIC TRANSPORT

Internal flights Services throughout the country are provided by Alitalia – the national airline (☎ 06/2222; www.alitalia.it) and smaller companies such as Meridiana, which flies to Perétola airport. Flights to Florence from Rome are 75 minutes; Milan 60 minutes.

Trains Italian State Railways (Trenitalia; www.trenitalia.it) provides a well-run and inexpensive service. Florence is the hub of the Tuscan rail network, with good connections with Pisa, Arezzo, Lucca and Viareggio. The train is more comfortable than a bus but less frequent. There are two classes of travel: first and second.

Regional buses There is no national bus company, though Lazzi (☎ 055/363 041; www.lazzi.it) and SITA (☎ 055/47 821; www.sitabus.it) have a major presence in Tuscany. Bus terminals in larger towns are often next to the rail station; in smaller towns most buses pull in at the central piazza.

Ferries Tuscany has three main ferry ports: Livorno serves Corsica, Sardinia, Sicily and the Tuscan Archipelago. Piombino has services to Elba, connecting to Portoferraio and Corsica, plus the smaller ports of Cavo and Rio Marina. Porto Santo Stefano has ferries to Corsica and Giglio.

Urban transport City buses are inexpensive, charging a flat fare. Invariably you need a ticket before getting on. Buy them in *tabacchi* or from kiosks at bus terminals and stops. In Florence most routes pass by the station. Validate tickets on boarding. The service is reasonably frequent, but buses can get very crowded in rush hours. For more details contact ATAF ☎ 800 425 500 (free call within Italy); www.ataf.net.

TAXIS

Taxis are available in all towns and tourist resorts. Taxis can be hailed, though you will be lucky to find one passing when you want one. Otherwise find a taxi stand (usually at stations and major *piazze*), or call a radio taxi (in Florence ☎ 055/4390 or 055/4798).

DRIVING

- The Italians drive on the right side of the road.
- Seat belts must be worn in front seats at all times and in rear seats where fitted.
- Random breath-testing takes place. Never drive under the influence of alcohol.
- Fuel is more expensive in Italy than in Britain and most other European countries, but diesel tends to be slightly less expensive. All except garages in rural places sell unleaded fuel *(senza piombo)*. Outside urban areas fuel stations usually open 7am to 12:30pm and 3 to 7:30pm. Credit cards are rarely accepted.
- Speed limits are as follows: toll-operated motorways *(autostrade)*: 130kph (80mph); main roads: 110kph (68mph); secondary roads: 90kph (55mph); urban roads: 50kph (31mph).
- In the event of a breakdown, you can call 803 116, giving your registration number and type of car, and the nearest ACI (Automobile Club d'Italia) office will assist you. You will be towed to the nearest ACI garage. This service is free to cars rented from Rome or Milan airport (you will need to produce your passport). If you are driving a rental car, call the emergency number in your documentation.

CAR RENTAL

Car rental is available in most cities and resorts from international and Italian companies but is expensive. Generally small local firms offer better rates but cars can only be reserved locally. Air or train travellers can take advantage of special inclusive deals.

FARES AND CONCESSIONS

Holders of an International Student Identity Card (ISIC) can take advantage of discounts offered to travelling students. Those under 26 who are not students can obtain an International Youth Card from student organizations that entitles the holder to discounts on transport, accommodation and museums. Citizens aged over 60 (and under 18) of EU and a number of other countries with which Italy has a reciprocal arrangement (not including the USA) may gain free admission to communal and state museums and receive discounts at other museums and on public transport on production of their passport.

Being there

TOURIST OFFICES

Arezzo
Piazza della Repubblica 28
☎ 0575/377 678,
www.apt.arezzo.it

Cortona
Palazzo Casali,
Piazza Signorelli
☎ 0575/637 221

Florence
Via Cavour 1r
☎ 055/290 832;
Borgo Santa Croce 29r
☎ 055/234 0444;
Piazza della Stazione 4/A
☎ 055/212 245;
www.firenzeturismo.it

Lucca
Piazzale Giuseppe Verdi
☎ 0583/442 944,
www.luccaturismo.it

Pisa
Piazza Arcivescadovo
☎ 050/42 291,
www.pisaturismo.it

Pistoia
Piazza del Duomo 4
☎ 0573/21 622,
www.pistoia.turismo.toscana.it

San Gimignano
Piazza del Duomo
☎ 0577/940 008

Siena
Piazza del Campo 56
☎ 0577/280 551,
www.terresiena.it

Viareggio
Viale G Carducci 10
☎ 0584/962 233

MONEY

The euro (€) is the official currency of Italy. Banknotes are issued in denominations of 5, 10, 20, 50, 100, 200 and 500 euros; coins in denominations of 1, 2, 5, 10, 20 and 50 cents, and 1 and 2 euros.

ELECTRICITY

The power supply is 220 volts. Round two- or three-hole sockets take plugs of two round pins or sometimes three pins in a vertical row. British visitors should bring an adaptor; US visitors a voltage transformer.

TIPS/GRATUITIES

Yes ✓   No ✗

Restaurants (if service not included)	✓ 10–15%
Cafés/bars (if service not included)	✓ €1 minimum
Taxis (short journeys)	✓ Round up to nearest euro
Porters	✓ €1
Chambermaids	✓ 50c–€1 per day
Toilet attendants	✓ 10c min

POSTAL SERVICES

The Italian postal system can be notoriously slow. In Florence the central post office is at Via Pellicceria 8. Post offices in cities and major towns open Mon–Sat 8:15–7, other offices open Mon–Fri 8:15–1:30, Sat 8:15am–12:30pm. Closed Sun ☎ 055/273 6481; www.poste.it.

TELEPHONES

Almost every bar in Italy has a telephone, plus there are many in public places. Tokens and phonecards are available from Telecom Italia offices, tobacconists, stations and other outlets.

International dialling codes

From Italy to:
UK: 00 44
Germany: 00 49

USA: 00 1
Netherlands: 00 31
Spain: 00 34

Emergency telephone numbers

Any emergency/*Carabinieri*: 112
Police: 113
Fire: 115

Medical emergency: 118
Road Assistance (ACI): 803 116

EMBASSIES AND CONSULATES

UK ☎ 055/284 133 (Florence)
Germany ☎ 055/234 3543 (Florence)
USA ☎ 055/266 951 (Florence)

Netherlands ☎ 055/475 249 (Florence)
Spain ☎ 06 684 0401 (Rome)

HEALTH ADVICE

Sun advice A sunscreen is recommended at all times.

Drugs Pharmacies *(farmacia)*, recognized by their green cross sign, possess highly trained staff able to offer medical advice on minor ailments and provide a wide range of prescribed and non-prescribed medicines and drugs.

Safe water It is quite safe to drink tap water and water from drinking fountains, but never drink from a tap marked *acqua non potabile*. However, many Italians prefer the taste of bottled mineral water, which is widely available.

PERSONAL SAFETY

The *Carabinieri* (military-style uniforms and white shoulder belts) deal with general crime and public order. Tuscans are generally law-abiding. Petty theft is the main problem (bag-snatching, pickpocketing and car break-ins). Some precautions:

● Carry shoulder bags not *on* your shoulder but slung *across* your body.
● Scooter-borne bag-snatchers can be foiled if you keep well away from the edge of the road.
● Do not put anything down on a café or restaurant table.
● Lock car doors and never keep valuables in your car.

OPENING HOURS

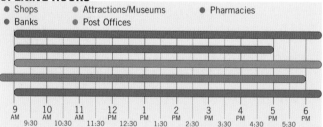

Some shops are closed Monday morning, others on Saturday afternoon or all day Saturday. Some close 1–4 every afternoon for siesta. Nearly all shops close Sunday, except in Florence and major tourist resorts. Bank afternoon opening times vary but all are closed weekends. Museum times also vary. Museums often close early on Sunday (around noon) and most close on Monday. Minor post offices open mornings only. Restaurants generally serve lunch 12–3 and dinner 7:30–11.

LANGUAGE

The Tuscan dialect is the purest form of spoken Italian. Many Italians speak English, but you will be better received if you at least attempt to communicate in Italian. Italian words are pronounced phonetically. Every vowel and consonant (except 'h') is sounded. The accent usually (but not always) falls on the penultimate syllable. Below is a list of a few words that may be helpful. More extensive coverage can be found in the AA's *Essential Italian Phrase Book*, which lists 2,000 phrases and 2,000 words.

yes	*sì*	help!	*aiuto!*
no	*no*	today	*oggi*
please	*per favore*	tomorrow	*domani*
thank you	*grazie*	yesterday	*ieri*
hello	*ciao*	how much?	*quanto?*
goodbye	*arrivederci*	expensive	*caro*
goodnight	*buona notte*	open	*aperto*
sorry	*mi dispiace*	closed	*chiuso*
hotel	*albergo*	reservation	*prenotazione*
room	*camera*	rate	*tariffa*
..single/double	*..singola/doppia*	breakfast	*prima colazione*
..one/two nights	*per una/due notte/i*	toilet/bath/shower	*toilette/bagno/ doccia*
..one/two people	*..per una/due persona/e*	key	*chiave*
restaurant	*ristorante*	lunch	*pranzo/colazione*
café	*caffè*	dinner	*cena*
table	*tavolo*	starter	*il primo*
menu	*menù/carta*	main course	*il secondo*
set menu	*menù turistico*	dish of the day	*piatto del giorno*
wine list	*lista dei vini*	dessert	*dolci*
aeroplane	*aeroplano*	ferry	*traghetto*
airport	*aeroporto*	ticket	*biglietto*
train	*treno*	ticket office	*biglietteria*
bus	*autobus*	timetable	*orario*

Best places to see

1 Cappelle Medicee

The Medici's private chapels and mausoleum feature several of Michelangelo's most outstanding pieces of Florentine funerary sculpture.

The Medici Chapels consist of the Crypt, a mausoleum for minor members of the Medici; the Cappella dei Principi, a vast and opulent chapel dedicated to six of the Medici Grand Dukes; and the Sagrestia Nuova, the last resting place of four of the family's leading lights.

The Crypt is the least interesting area, its dour, low-ceilinged vaults dotted with the brass-railed tombs of 49 lesser Medici. All were buried pell-mell in 1791 by Ferdinand III, only to be exhumed and re-buried in a more dignified manner in 1857. Steps lead from here to the Cappella dei Principi, begun as a family mausoleum for Cosimo I in 1604. A riot of decoration, this vast, marble-lined chapel was the most expensive project ever commissioned by the Medici. Around the walls, 16 coats of arms represent Medici-controlled Tuscan towns.

A corridor leads to the Sagrestia Nuova (New Sacristy), designed as a contrast to Brunelleschi's Old Sacristy in nearby San Lorenzo. It contains three groups of sculpture (1520–34), two wholly and one partly by Michelangelo. On the left is the

tomb of Lorenzo, grandson of Lorenzo the Magnificent, whose statue symbolizes the contemplative life. On the right stands the tomb of Giuliano, third son of Lorenzo the Magnificent, symbolizing the active life. The third (unfinished) group – a Madonna and Child – was intended as the tomb of Lorenzo the Magnificent and his brother Giuliano.

www.polomuseale.firenze.it/english

✚ *Firenze 4b*

✉ Piazza Madonna degli Aldobrandini, Florence

☎ 055/238 8602; advance reservation 055/294 883

🕐 Tue–Sun 8:15–1:50 (also 2nd and 4th Mon of month). Closed 2nd and 4th Sun of month ✋ Expensive

🚌 In the pedestrian zone: nearest service 1, 6, 7

❓ Visit in conjunction with San Lorenzo (➤ 112)

2 Collegiata di San Gimignano

A series of superbly preserved medieval frescoes almost completely covers San Gimignano's most important church.

Most people visit San Gimignano for its 13 famous medieval towers (▶ 162–163), only to find that the most memorable part of their visit is the fresco-covered Collegiata, a church which served as the village's cathedral until San Gimignano ceased to be a bishopric. Begun in 1148, but later enlarged, it has little in its simple Romanesque façade to prepare you for the decorative wonder inside. Tuscany is filled with fresco cycles, and those in the Collegiata

HOC OPVS FIERI FECIT · IVLIANVS QVONDAM
MARTINI CETTI DE SCO GEMINIANO · M·CCC·

are not necessarily the region's most famous, but few cycles are as extensive, and few have the charm of these. The first panels, by Taddeo di Bartolo, fill the church's back wall and depict the Last Judgement (1393), with Paradise and Hell portrayed on two adjoining walls. Below is a large St Sebastian by Benozzo Gozzoli (1420–97).

On the church's right-hand (south) wall is a 22-panel cycle attributed to Lippo Memmi, a 14th-century Sienese artist, which depicts various New Testament scenes from the Passion and the Life of Christ. On the opposite wall are 26 panels (completed in 1367) by Bartolo di Fredi, a cycle of Old Testament episodes including scenes from the stories of Genesis, Abraham, Joseph, Moses and Job. To the left of the high altar, the Cappella di San Gimignano has a fine altar (1475) by Benedetto da Maiano, the sculptor responsible for the altar, marble shrine and bas-reliefs in the Cappella di Santa Fina (top of the right aisle). This chapel is better known for its fresco cycle by Domenico Ghirlandaio (1449–94), another artist whose work reflects the tone and life of his own period. This cycle depicts the Life of St Fina, one of San Gimignano's patron saints. Look for the fresco that features a 15th-century view of the town.

✚ 17J ✉ Piazza del Duomo 1, San Gimignano
☎ 0577/940 316 🕐 Church and Cappella di Santa Fina: Apr–Oct Mon–Fri 9:30–7:10, Sat 9:30–5:10, Sun 12:30–5:10; Mar, Nov to mid-Jan Mon–Sat 9:30–4:40, Sun 12:30–4:40; mid-Jan to Feb closed except for services. Check with tourist office 🖑 Moderate 🍴 In Piazza della Cisterna (€–€€) 🚌 In the pedestrian zone

David

Michelangelo's celebrated statue is one of the most familiar of all Renaissance images, and one of the essential sights of any visit to Florence.

Michelangelo's *David* is exhibited in the Galleria dell'Accademia, Europe's first artistic academy (founded in 1563), together with five other Michelangelo statues and an interesting collection of Gothic and Renaissance paintings. Italy's most famous sculpture was commissioned by the Opera del Duomo in 1501, when Michelangelo was just 26. Its theme – David defeating the tyrant Goliath – was chosen to symbolize the virtues of Florence (then a republic), its freedom from papal and foreign domination, and its recent liberation from Savonarola and the Medici. The marble

from which it was sculpted, a vast 5m (16ft) block, had been quarried from Carrara some 40 years earlier but was so thin and riddled with cracks that it had defied the ambitions of all other sculptors. In Michelangelo's hands, however, it was transformed in just three years into a work that secured his reputation as the foremost sculptor of his day.

When it was completed, 30 leading artists were asked to select a site for the statue. The Piazza della Signoria was their eventual choice. There *David* remained, ravaged by wind and rain, until 1873. The fact that the figure was intended as a piece of outdoor sculpture helps to explain its famous distortions – notably the over-large hands and face – features designed to emphasize its monumentality.

Elsewhere in the gallery are Michelangelo's *St Matthew* (1504–8) and four unfinished *Slaves*, or *Prisoners* (1521–3), the latter a graphic illustration of Michelangelo's dictum that sculpture was the liberation of a form that was already 'imprisoned' in the stone. There are also paintings by Botticelli, Perugino, Pontormo, Filippino Lippi and others.

www.polomuseale.firenze.it/english
✚ *Firenze 6a* ✉ Via Ricasoli 60, Florence ☎ 055/238 8609; advance reservation 055/294 883 🕐 Tue–Sun 8:15–6:50 💰 Expensive 🍴 In Piazza San Marco and Via del Ricasoli (€) 🚌 1, 6, 7, 11, C and other services to San Marco

4 Duomo di Siena

This magnificent Gothic cathedral has one of Italy's loveliest façades and an interior bursting with outstanding works of art.

Siena's cathedral was begun in 1196 and completed in 1376, during which time there was an aborted attempt to extend the building, a scheme whose half-finished results can be seen in the skeletal shell to the right of the present structure. Much of the lower part of the façade (1285) was designed by Giovanni Pisano, though most of his original statuary is now in the nearby Museo dell'Opera.

The exterior's distinctive black-and-white banding is echoed in the interior's monochrome floor, which consists of 56 panels (1349–1547) created over the centuries by some of Siena's leading artists. Midway down the left aisle (fourth altar) stands the Piccolomini altar, whose four lower-niche statues are early works by Michelangelo. Alongside lies the entrance to the Libreria Piccolomini, beautifully frescoed by Pinturicchio with scenes from the life of Aeneas Piccolomini (1509), a Tuscan nobleman who became Pope Pius II.

At the end of the left aisle stands the Duomo's masterpiece: Nicola Pisano's Gothic pulpit (1268). To its left, in the corner chapel, is Tino da Camaino's influential Tomb of Cardinal Petroni (1318). Below it lies Donatello's bronze floor tomb of Bishop Pecci (1426). The circular Cappella di San Giovanni in the left transept has a bronze statue of John the Baptist by Donatello and more Pinturicchio frescoes. A similar chapel in the opposite transept, the Cappella Chigi, was designed by Bernini. Be sure to visit the Baptistery, to the rear of the cathedral, which

features swathes of lovely 15th-century frescoes
and a font with bronze panels by Ghiberti, Donatello
and Jacopo della Quercia.

www.operaduomo.siena.it

🞤 19K 🖂 Piazza del Duomo, Siena ☎ 0577/283 048
🕔 Duomo: Mar–late Aug Mon–Sat 10:30–7:30, Sun
1:30–7:30; late Aug–Oct daily 9:30–7:30; late Oct–Feb
Mon–Sat 10:30–6:30, Sun 1:30–6:30 💶 Duomo (includes
Libreria Piccolomini): inexpensive Nov–Jul, when the ornate
floor is covered; expensive Aug–Oct. Baptistery: inexpensive
🚌 In the pedestrian zone: occasional shuttle bus services

5 Galleria degli Uffizi

One of the world's finest art galleries, the Uffizi contains a collection of paintings that features all the great names of the Florentine Renaissance.

The building housing the Uffizi was begun by Vasari in 1560, its original purpose being to serve as a suite of offices *(uffizi)* from which the Medici could administer the Grand Duchy of Tuscany. In 1737 it was bequeathed to Florence, along with the Medici art collection, by Anna Luisa, sister of Gian Gastone, the last Medici Grand Duke. Today its 45 rooms house not only the cream of 14th- and 15th-century Florentine paintings, but also masterpieces from elsewhere in Italy (notably Venice and Siena), together with a surprising

number of major works from Germany, Holland and Spain. Rooms 1–15 are given over to the Florentine Renaissance (and contain the most famous paintings); rooms 16–27 concentrate on the age of High Renaissance and Mannerism, and rooms 28–45 are devoted to later Italian and European paintings.

Highlights are too numerous to mention, though certain works deserve extra special attention. Room 2 opens with altarpieces of the *Maestà (Madonna Enthroned)* by Giotto, Duccio and Cimabue, three of Italy's greatest 13th-century painters, who contributed to the movement towards naturalism and

emotion and away from the stilted and more stylized Byzantine approach to subjects in art. Room 3's Sienese paintings are dominated by Simone Martini's sublime *Annunciation*, while in rooms 5 and 6 the key work is Gentile da Fabriano's exquisitely detailed *Adoration of the Magi*. Rooms 10–14 feature paintings by Botticelli, notably the famous *Primavera* and *Birth of Venus*. Room 18 is best known for the *Venus de' Medici*, renowned for centuries as one of antiquity's most erotic statues. Successive rooms feature works by, among others, Raphael, Caravaggio and Michelangelo; the Venetians Titian, Giorgione and Carpaccio; and Europeans such as Rembrandt, Rubens and Van Dyck.

www.polomuseale.firenze.it/english
🕂 *Firenze 5e* ✉ Loggiato degli Uffizi 6, off Piazza della Signoria, Florence ☎ 055/238 8651 🕐 Tue–Sun 8:15–6:50 (ticket office closes 45 mins earlier). Closed Mon, 1 Jan, Easter Sun, 1 May, 15 Aug, 25 Dec 🕙 Expensive 🍴 Café (€) 🚻 B ❓ Tickets can be reserved for admission at a set time to the Uffizi and other museums by calling Firenze Musei 055/294 883

6 Museo Nazionale del Bargello

Italy's greatest collection of Renaissance sculpture is contained in the Bargello, together with an array of majolica, tapestries, paintings and silverware.

The fortress-like Bargello, begun in 1255, was Florence's earliest civic palace, serving first as the city's seat of government and later as the home of the chief of police. Later still it became a prison, torture chamber and place of execution, assuming its present role in 1865. The museum spreads over three floors, though its key works are found in just two large rooms. The first lies to the right of the

ticket hall, and concentrates on the late Renaissance works of Michelangelo, Giambologna and Benvenuto Cellini. Michelangelo is represented by three contrasting works: a delicate tondo (circular artwork) of the Madonna and Child; a powerful portrait bust of Brutus; and a lurching, soft-bellied statue of Bacchus. Other highlights include a bronze of Cosimo I by Cellini and Giambologna's celebrated Mercury, a sublime study in speed.

From this first room, wander into the courtyard, glance at the exterior sculptures in the small rooms opposite, then climb the external staircase to the first floor. At the top of the stairs is a wonderful menagerie of bronze animals by Giambologna. Turn right for the museum's second major room, a glorious vaulted hall filled with sculptural masterpieces. Look in particular for the works of Donatello, notably his St George, removed from Orsanmichele; the Marzocco, Florence's heraldic lion; and the debonair and famously androgynous statue of David. Subsequent rooms are crammed with rugs, tapestries, glassware, silverware and other precious objets d'art. Particularly noteworthy is the Salone del Camino, with Italy's most important collection of small bronzes.

www.polomuseale.firenze.it/english

➕ *Firenze 6d* ✉ Via del Proconsolo 4, Florence ☎ 055/238 8606; advance reservation 055/294 883 🕐 Daily 8:15–2. Closed 1st, 3rd, 5th Sun and 2nd, 4th Mon of month
✋ Moderate 🍴 Via del Proconsolo (€) 🚌 19, A

7 Museo di San Marco

The ancient Dominican convent of San Marco is renowned for a series of sublime frescoes and paintings by Fra Angelico.

San Marco was originally owned by Vallombrosan and Sylvestrine monks, passing to the Dominicans in 1436, when it was restored at Cosimo de' Medici's personal expense. Its subsequent priors included Fra Angelico, not only a devout Dominican,

but also one of the finest of Florence's early Renaissance painters. Today the convent buildings are a museum given over almost entirely to the artist's paintings and frescoes.

Many of the paintings are contained in the Ospizio dei Pellegrini, a room once used to provide pilgrims with food and shelter (located off the main cloister). Its two masterpieces hang on opposite walls: a Deposition (1440), removed from the church of Santa Trinità, and the Madonna dei Linaiuoli (1433), commissioned for the headquarters of the flax-makers' *(linaiuoli)* guild. Also off the cloister is the Sala Capitolare, or Chapter House, which features a Crucifixion (1442) by Fra Angelico. The Refectory nearby contains a large fresco of the Last Supper by Domenico Ghirlandaio (beyond the shop).

On the first floor you are greeted by Fra Angelico's famous *Annunciation* (c1445), one of the most beautiful of all Renaissance paintings. The rest of the floor is largely taken up by 44 dormitory cells, each frescoed by Fra Angelico and his pupils with

religious scenes intended as aids to monastic devotion. At the end of the far corridor are three cells once occupied by Savonarola. At the end of the corridor on your right are two cells, larger than the rest, once used by Cosimo il Vecchio de' Medici. Close by is Europe's first public library, designed for Cosimo by Michelozzo in 1441.

www.polomuseale.firenze.it/english

✚ *Firenze 6a* ✉ Piazza San Marco, Florence ☎ 055/238 8608; advance reservations 055/294 883 🕐 Mon–Fri 8:30–1:50, Sat 8:15/30–6:50, Sun 8:15/30–7. Closed 1st, 3rd, 5th Sun and 2nd, 4th Mon of month ✋ Moderate 🍴 In Piazza San Marco (€) 🚌 1, 6, 7, 10, 11, 17, 20, 25, 31, 32, 33, C

8 Piazza del Campo

Siena's magnificent central piazza and its arc of rosy palaces make up one of Europe's most beautiful medieval squares.

Walking into the Campo from Siena's tight huddle of streets is like stepping onto some medieval stage set. Situated at the heart of the old city, the conch-shaped piazza resembles a vast amphitheatre, its broad sweep of palaces culminating in the battlemented grandeur of the Palazzo Pubblico and its attendant bell tower.

The square probably began life as the Roman forum, becoming the town's principal marketplace before taking on its present form in 1293, when the Council of Nine, Siena's governing body, began to buy up land with a view to creating a great central square. The carefully chosen area was at the heart of Siena's *terzi* (the city's three main districts), and was the only piece of land

owned by none of Siena's *contrade*, the city's fiercely competitive medieval parishes. As such the Council hoped the square would become the focus of civic life, a physical expression of good government, and a symbol of citizens' loyalty to Siena rather than to factions, families, *terzi* or *contrade*.

The Campo was completed in 1349 with the addition of its brick

paving, whose nine sections were designed to symbolize the Council of Nine, and the folds of the Virgin's cloak, sheltering the city under its protective embrace. Both the Palazzo Pubblico and Torre del Mangia are well worth visiting, but you should also indulge in at least one pricey cappuccino at one of the Campo's cafés, an ideal way to take in the square's endless street life. Be warned, however, most of the restaurants are very expensive.

➕ 19K ✉ Piazza del Campo, Siena ☎ None 🕐 Daily 24 hours 👆 Free 🍴 Il Campo (€€€; ➤ 182) 🚌 In the pedestrian zone

Santa Croce

The most famous church in Florence is celebrated for its superb Giotto frescoes and the tombs of Galileo, Michelangelo and Machiavelli.

Begun in 1294 by Arnolfo di Cambio, and completed in 1450, this Franciscan foundation attracted the attention of many wealthy families, all anxious to seek spiritual salvation by being buried among the 'humble' Franciscans; hence the many tombs and the various frescoed family chapels (notably those of the Bardi, Peruzzi and Baroncelli).

Among those buried in the church are Michelangelo (first tomb on the right), Machiavelli (sixth on the right) and Galileo (first on the left). There are also outstanding examples of Renaissance funerary sculpture, notably 15th-century works by Bernardo Rossellino (end of the right aisle) and Desiderio da Settignano (end of the left aisle). More famous still are the church's fresco cycles, the best known of which are by Giotto, who was responsible for the paintings in the Cappella Bardi and the Cappella Peruzzi (adjacent chapels to the right of the high altar).

To the right of the church lie the Cappella dei Pazzi (1430) and the Museo dell'Opera di Santa Croce. The former, rather austere chapel by Brunelleschi, is simply decorated with 12 terracotta tondi of the Apostles by Luca della Robbia, who also decorated the portico and polychrome roundels in the upper corners (attributed to Brunelleschi and Donatello). The Museo's highlights are Donatello's St Louise of Toulouse and a crucifix by Cimabue.

www.santacroce.firenze.it

✚ *Firenze 7e* ✉ Piazza Santa Croce, Florence ☎ 055/246 6105 🕐 Mon–Sat 9:30–5:30, Sun 1–5:30; may open later in summer 🎟 Church: moderate; includes Museo dell'Opera di Santa Croce and Cappella dei Pazzi 🚌 13, 23, B, C

10 Torre Pendente

Few sights are as immediately recognizable as the Leaning Tower of Pisa, one of several monuments in Pisa's beautiful Campo dei Miracoli.

Pisa's famous tower was begun in 1173 as a companion for the city's Duomo and Baptistery, two buildings that make up a lovely medieval ensemble in a green-lawned square known as the Campo dei Miracoli ('Field of Miracles'). The tower began to lean almost from the outset, tilting into the sandy subsoil under the foundations (this part of the coast was once under water, so local soil is composed almost entirely of sand and silt). Initial construction work on the tower was abandoned after only three storeys were complete, but work resumed in the 13th century, when it was accepted that the tower would not fall. Over the next 180 years a series of architects tried to correct the lean by adding off-centre sections. None was successful. At its worst, the tower was a dizzying 4.5m (15ft) to the vertical.

Architects agonized over how to prevent the tower's collapse and reverse the lean. Many schemes were put forward, but none was taken seriously until the tower was closed to the public in 1990 after it was deemed to have become dangerous. Over the next few years, some 900 tonnes of lead were strapped to the tower's base on its northern side to help counter the lean. By 1998 some improvement had been seen, and a delicate drilling operation began to remove water and subsoil from the tower's northern foundations. The drying of the soil and the removal of material created a gradual subsidence on one side of the tower, which saw the lean corrected by around 10 per cent, bringing it to the angle it had in 1838. The project cost more than £20 million and took 11 years to complete.

www.opapisa.it

✚ 13G ✉ Campo (Piazza) dei Miracoli, Pisa ☎ To prebook tours: 050/506 547; www.opapisa.it ◷ Mid-Jun to Aug daily 8:30am–11pm; Apr to mid-Jun, Sep 8:30–8:30; Oct 9–7; Nov to late Dec, early Jan–Feb 10–5; end Dec–early Jan 9–6 💰 Expensive 🚌 1 from rail station ❓ Prebooking is recommended

Best things to do

Good places to have lunch

Following is a selection of places to eat in Florence (Firenze) where you should be able to get a good meal and a little bit of local atmosphere.

Antellesi (€–€€)

An easygoing place with wooden tables and traditional dishes.
✉ Via Faenza 9r ☎ 055/216 990

Baldovino (€€)

A relaxed atmosphere and convenient for Santa Croce.
✉ Via San Giuseppe 2r ☎ 055/241 773; www.baldovino.com

Belle Donne (€–€€)

A friendly restaurant with shared tables and an eye-catching interior.

✉ Via delle Belle Donne 16r ☎ 055/238 2609

Cantinetta Antinori (€€€)

Elegant and beautiful wine bar with a lively atmosphere.

✉ Piazza Antinori 3 ☎ 055/292 234; www.cantinetta-antinori.com

Cantinetta dei Verrazzano (€€)

Nice wine bar with marble-topped tables and tasty Tuscan snacks.

✉ Via dei Tavolini 18–20r ☎ 055/268 590

Il Cantinone del Gallo Nero (€)

Wine bar in a vaulted cellar with a choice of starters and hot and cold snacks.

✉ Via Santo Spirito 6r ☎ 055/218 898 🕐 Closed Mon

Cibreo (€€)

Have lunch in the less expensive bistro to the rear of the main restaurant.

✉ Via del Verrocchio 8r ☎ 055/234 1100; www.fabiopicchi.it

Da Ganino (€–€€)

Central, reasonably priced restaurant with outside tables.

✉ Piazza dei Cimatori 4r ☎ 055/214 125

Latini (€)

A busy trattoria with crowded tables and a raucous atmosphere.

✉ Via dei Palchetti, off Via della Vigna Nuova ☎ 055/210 916; www.illatini.com 🕐 Closed Mon

Le Volpi e L'Uva (€–€€)

A delightful wine bar with a wide variety of wines and cold snacks.

✉ Piazza dei Rossi 1r ☎ 055/239 8132; www.levolpieluva.com 🕐 Closed Sun

Top activities

Bicycling Bicycles can be rented in Florence and most large towns. Contact individual tourist offices for details.

Canoeing For information contact the Federazione Italiana Canoa (☎ 055/689 044; www.federcanoa.it).

Caving Excellent opportunities in the Alpi Apuane: contact Gruppo Speleologico Fiorentino (☎ 055/660 754; www.gsfi.da.ru).

Diving Off the coast and islands of the Tuscan Archipelago: contact the Federazione Italiana Attività Subacquee (FIAS), www.fipsas.it.

Fishing Plenty of coastal and sea fishing; contact local tourist offices for details of conditions, permits and tackle shops.

Horse-back riding Riding and pony-trekking are widely available throughout Tuscany: most tourist offices carry lists of local venues.

Mountaineering In the Alpi Apuane, Orecchiella and elsewhere. Most towns have a branch office of the Club Alpino Italiano (CAI): contact tourist offices for local addresses. The Florence office is at Via del Mezzetta 2/M (☎ 055/612 0467; www.caifirenze.it).

Skiing Winter sports are available, snow allowing, around Abetone, to the northeast of Lucca.

Walking Several companies organize walking tours in Florence. Try www.italy.artviva.com, www.florenceguides.it or www.city-sightseeing.it.

Windsurfing Off the coast and islands of the Tuscan archipelago, notably Elba. Contact the Associazione Surfisti Italiani Versilia, Via Nino Bixio 30, Viareggio (LU), Tuscany (☎ 0584 55 074).

Stunning views

From the Campanile, Florence (➤ 80–81).

From the Fortezza, Montalcino (➤ 157–158).

From the Fortezza Medicea, Cortona (➤ 156).

From Piazzale Michelangelo, Florence (➤ 93).

From Santa Maria dei Servi, Siena (➤ 173).

From the Torre Grossa, San Gimignano (► 163).

From the Torre Guinigi, Lucca (► 143).

From the Torre del Mangia in the Palazzo Pubblico, Siena (► 169).

From the Torre Pendente (Leaning Tower), Pisa (► 54–55).

From the walls of the hilltop village of Pienza (► 160–161).

Great shopping in Florence

FOOD AND WINE
Pegna
Pegna has been in the business of selling mouth-watering food since 1860. The supermarket layout is a boon for those whose Italian may not be up to ordering in small delicatessens.

✉ Via dello Studio 26r ☎ 055/282 701; www.pegna.it 🚌 In pedestrian zone

LEATHER GOODS
Cellerini
Most Florentines wanting a bag make straight for this famous store. Some 600 different types of handbag and other luggage hang from the Renaissance ceiling of the 16th-century *palazzo* in which the shop is housed.

✉ Via del Sole 37r, off Via della Spada ☎ 055/282 533; www.cellerini.it
🚌 6, 11, B

PAPER AND STATIONERY
Il Papiro
Papiro is a chain of stationers selling marbled paper and marbled paper goods at lower prices than the city's more famous names.

✉ Via dei Tavolini 13r, off Via dei Calzaiuoli ☎ 055/213 823 🚌 In the pedestrian zone ✉ Via Cavour 55r ☎ 055/215 262; www.ilpapirofirenze.it
🚌 1, 6, 7

Pineider
This celebrated stationery shop has been here since 1774. Byron, Shelley, Puccini, Stendhal, Napoleon and Maria Callas are just a few of the famous who have corresponded on this paper. Elizabeth Taylor ordered visiting cards from the company to match her eyes.

✉ Piazza della Signoria 13r ☎ 055/284 655 🚌 B (in the pedestrian zone)

PRINTS
Giovanni Baccani
There are shops selling prints, engravings and paintings in every

corner of the city, but the selection at this charming store, established in 1903, is so good that you won't need to go elsewhere. Prices range from very reasonable to very prohibitive.

✉ Via della Vigna Nuova 75r ☎ 055/214 467 🚌 6, 11, 31, 32

SHOES
Salvatore Ferragamo

This famous name has its origins planted in Florence. The city's flagship store contains a fascinating museum dedicated to the exquisite shoes made by the company over the years.

✉ Via dei Tornabuoni 14r ☎ 055/292 123; www.salvatoreferragamo.com
🚌 6, 11, A

Best Tuscan hill towns

Arezzo The highlight of eastern Tuscany, known for its jewellery and Piero della Francesca fresco cycle (➤ 154–155).

Colle di Val d'Elsa A tiny and often-overlooked village known for its glassware (➤ 166).

Cortona Glorious views and steep, atmospheric streets are Cortona's main attractions (➤ 156–157).

Montalcino A delightful small town at the heart of ravishing wine country (➤ 157–158).

Montepulciano One of the loftiest of Tuscany's many hill towns (➤ 158–159).

Monteriggioni Towers and a ring of walls make this one of Italy's best-preserved medieval villages (▶ 166).

Pienza A tiny Renaissance jewel at the heart of divine countryside (▶ 160).

San Gimignano No other hill town looks as impressive from afar as this many-towered 'medieval Manhattan' (▶ 162–165).

Siena Filled with sublime art and architecture, this is one of Italy's finest historic towns (▶ 168–173).

Volterra A remote, Etruscan town that commands views over an eerie, bare-hilled landscape (▶ 176).

Places to take the children

FLORENCE
Ice cream
Few children will be able to resist an ice cream or *granita* (crushed ice with a choice of fruit syrup). Good places to visit include:
Carabé (€) ✉ Via Ricasoli 60r ☎ 055/289 476
Festival del Gelato (€) ✉ Via del Corso 75r ☎ 055/294 386
Perché No! (€) ✉ Via dei Tavolini 19r ☎ 055/239 8969
Vivoli (€) ✉ Via Isole delle Stinche 7r ☎ 055/292 334

Galleries and museums
Children might enjoy a small dose of carefully chosen culture. Michelangelo's *David* is a good place to start (➤ 40–41). The detailed narrative of Gozzoli's frescoes in the Palazzo Medici-Riccardi may captivate, as may the frescoes of Fra Angelico in San Marco (➤ 48–49). The armour and Giambologna's menagerie in the Bargello should also be popular (➤ 46–47). Interesting museums include the Museo di Storia della Scienza (➤ 96–97), Museo dei Ragazzi (in the Palazzo Vecchio, ➤ 105) and Museo della Casa Fiorentina Antica (➤ 89).

Sights
The tremendous view from the Campanile (➤ 80–81) should appeal to children, though you may well have trouble coaxing them up all the stairs (note that they may not enjoy the slightly claustrophobic passages of the cathedral dome).

TUSCANY
Beaches
The easiest beaches to reach from Florence are those of Viareggio, an elegant seaside resort about an hour from Florence on the train (regular seaside 'specials' run from the city in the summer). The sand is clean and the water safe, though many of the beaches are private – you pay a small fee to enjoy access to the sand, showers, bar and changing rooms. Further south, the (free) beach at Marina

di Alberese (21km/13 miles from Grosseto) is among the best in Tuscany, but is accessible only by car.

Sights

Views from the towers in San Gimignano (► 162–165), Siena (► 168–173) and Lucca (► 140–143) should appeal, along with the old walls and fortresses of Pienza (► 160), Montalcino (► 157–158) and Monteriggioni (► 166). The Leaning Tower of Pisa (► 54–55) will fascinate adults and children alike.

Museo Leonardiano

This interesting museum features beautiful models of Leonardo da Vinci's inventions from his notebooks.

✉ Castello dei Conti Guidi, Vinci (11km/ 7 miles north of Empoli) ☎ 0571/993 251; www.museoleonardiano.it 🕓 Daily 9:30–7 (6pm in winter) 🎫 Moderate

Parco di Pinocchio

The storybook character Pinocchio was created by Carlo Lorenzini (1826–90), who took his pen name from the village of Collodi, where his mother was born, 15km (9 miles) east of Lucca. The park has pretty walkways through woods. There are mosaics depicting episodes from Pinocchio's 'life', various monsters, sharks and tableaux, and a toy shop.

✉ Parco di Pinocchio, Collodi ☎ 0572/429 342; www.pinocchio.it 🕓 Daily 8–dusk 🎫 Expensive

a walk around Fiesole

The ancient hill town of Fiesole nestles in the hills above Florence, providing a tranquil retreat from the city during the dog days of summer. It is a popular destination on weekends, so be prepared for crowds.

Start in Piazza Mino da Fiesole and take Via Marini to the right of the Duomo to the Museo Bandini and archaeological zone.

The Cappella Salutati in the Duomo features two works by Mino da Fiesole: the *Tomb of Bishop Salutati* and an altar-frontal of the *Madonna and Child*. The cathedral's high altar has an impressive altarpiece by Bicci di Lorenzo. Off Via Marini lie the 1st-century BC Teatro Romano, the Museo Archeologico and the ruins of Etruscan walls and temples. The Antiquarium Costantini, in Via Portigiani, contains a fine collection of Greek vases. The Bandini museum houses early Florentine paintings. You can buy a combined ticket for the Museo Bandini, Antiquarium Costantini and Teatro Romano.

Return to Piazza Mino da Fiesole and take Via San Francesco off its northwest flank. Walk uphill to see San Francesco and Sant' Alessandro, returning to the piazza the way you came or via the parallel woodland path.

Sant'Alessandro, one of the town's loveliest buildings, was built in the 6th century over the site of Roman and Etruscan temples. San Francesco enjoys breezy views of Florence and has an important 15th-century painting, *The Immaculate Conception*, by Piero di Cosimo.

> *From the Piazza take Via Vecchia Fiesolana past the Villa Medici to San Domenico. Turn right on Via Badia dei Roccettini to the Badia Fiesolana.*

San Domenico contains a *Madonna and Child with Angels* (1430) by Fra Angelico; the chapter house (number 4) has a *Crucifixion* by the same artist. The Badia features a lovely 11th-century façade incorporated into a 15th-century frontage. Its interior is styled in the manner of Brunelleschi. This was Fiesole's original cathedral.

Distance 2.5km (1.5 miles) one way
Time Allow a morning
Start point Piazza Mino da Fiesole ✚ 10E
End point Badia Fiorentina or Piazza Mino da Fiesole ✚ 10E
🚌 7 ATAF bus from Florence rail station, Piazza San Marco or Via Martelli (near the Duomo) to Piazza Mino da Fiesole. Services call at San Domenico di Fiesole, near the Badia Fiesolana, for the return to Florence
🛈 Via Portigiani 3 ☎ 055/598 720; www.comune.fiesole.fi.it
Lunch Cafés around Piazza Mino da Fiesole (€)

Teatro Romano–Museo Archeologico
✉ Via Portigiani 1 ☎ 055/596 1293 🕐 Mar–Oct Mon–Sat 9–6, Sun 10–1, 2–6; Nov–Feb Mon–Sat 9–5, Sun 10–4 ♨ Moderate
❓ Museum ticket includes entrance to the Antiquarium Costantini

Museo Bandini
✉ Via Dupré 1 ☎ 055/596 1293 🕐 Apr–Sep Wed–Mon 10–7; Mar, Oct Wed–Mon 10–6; Nov–Feb Thu–Mon 10–4 ♨ Moderate

Best churches for art

Collegiata, San Gimignano Virtually every wall of this beguiling church is covered in superbly preserved medieval frescoes (➤ 38–39).

Duomo, Lucca One of Lucca's many captivating Romanesque churches, with exquisite sculpture and a fine façade (➤ 141).

Duomo, Siena Fresco cycles, medieval pulpits, sculpture by Donatello and much more fill the finest of Tuscany's many cathedrals (➤ 42–43).

Sant'Agostino, San Gimignano A fresco cycle by Benozzo Gozzoli dominates this church in a quiet corner of Tuscany's most celebrated hill town (➤ 165).

Sant'Antimo, near Montalcino Tuscany's loveliest Romanesque church occupies a beautiful pastoral setting (➤ 158).

Santa Croce, Florence Numerous tomb sculptures and frescoes by Giotto and others adorn Florence's most compelling church (➤ 52–53).

San Francesco, Arezzo This church contains Piero della Francesca's *Legend of the True Cross*, one of Italy's most important Renaissance fresco cycles (➤ 154).

San Lorenzo, Florence Brunelleschi's Renaissance masterpiece and adjoining Cappelle Medicee are graced with numerous important paintings and sculpture by Michelangelo and Donatello (➤ 112–114).

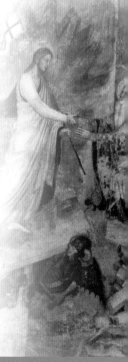

Santa Maria Novella, Florence A pioneering Renaissance masterpiece by Masaccio and several charming fresco cycles are just some of Santa Maria Novella's many artistic highlights (➤ 114–117).

San Miniato al Monte, Florence The city's most beautiful church contains a wealth of frescoes and an art-filled Renaissance chapel (➤ 118–119).

Exploring

Florence (Firenze) is one of the world's greatest artistic cities. A focal point for the Renaissance, one of history's most dramatic periods of creative endeavour, its churches, galleries and museums are filled with some of the finest art ever created. This said, not all your time should be spent admiring art. Florence has some superb shopping, from designer names to lively markets, and there are excellent bars, cafés and restaurants, as well as the simple charm of the city's medieval and Renaissance streets.

Tuscany, right on its doorstep, is one of Europe's most beautiful regions, a perfect patchwork of historic hill towns – notably Siena, Lucca and San Gimignano – sandy beaches, timeless pastoral countryside, jagged mountain peaks and much more. It provides a perfect escape from the hustle and bustle and, in summer, the sheer heat of Florence.

Florence

Florence is compact and easily explored on foot, though its wealth of art and culture, and the way sights are scattered across the city, make it difficult to plan convenient sightseeing itineraries. The historic heart conforms to the grid of the old Roman colony, its principal points of interest lying on and around two main squares: Piazza del Duomo and Piazza della Signoria.

Most people begin a tour of the city in Piazza del Duomo, where you should see the Duomo (cathedral), Baptistery and Museo dell'Opera, as well as climb the Campanile or cathedral dome for a superb view of the city. Close by lies the Museo Nazionale del Bargello, Italy's greatest collection of Renaissance sculpture. Via dei Calzaiuoli, Florence's pedestrianized main street, leads south to Piazza della Signoria, where you should visit the Palazzo Vecchio, the Uffizi and the nearby Museo di Storia della Scienza.

North of the central district the key sights are the Cappelle Medicee, with statues by Michelangelo, the Accademia (home to Michelangelo's *David*) and the Palazzo Medici-Riccardi, with its lovely fresco cycle. A little further north lies the Museo di San Marco, filled with sublime paintings by Fra Angelico. The city's two most important churches – Santa Croce and Santa Maria Novella –

lie east and west of the centre respectively. Across the Arno, the river that divides the city, is the quieter Oltrarno district, worth visiting for the Cappella Brancacci and its fresco cycle, and the Palazzo Pitti, home to a superb collection of Medici art and objects.

www.firenzeturismo.it

🚩 9E

ℹ️ Via Cavour 1r ☎ 055/290 832

BATTISTERO

The Baptistery of Florence was long believed to have been a
Roman temple to Mars; the disovery of floor fragments has
confirmed the existence of a 1st-century palace on the site,
though the core of the present building probably dates from the
6th to 7th centuries. The marble decoration of the classically
inspired exterior, remodelled in the 11th century, was to inspire
generations of architects and provide the model for countless
Tuscan churches.

The south doors (1330–36), the work of Andrea Pisano, depict scenes from the life of St John the Baptist (the patron saint of Florence), and were cast by Venetian bell makers, then Europe's most accomplished bronze smiths. A famous competition was arranged in 1401 to award the commission for the north doors (1403–24), an event widely considered to have marked the 'beginning' of the Renaissance. It was won by Lorenzo Ghiberti, also responsible for the east doors (1425–52), works so exquisite they are often known as the 'Gates of Paradise' (the original panels are now in the Museo dell'Opera, ➤ 94–95).

Inside, the highlights are the mosaic ceiling (begun in 1225), created by Venetian mosaicists, and the glorious tessellated marble floor, at whose heart you can still see the outlines of the building's original font (all Florentine children were once baptized here). Less eye-catching are the fine mosaic frieze; the lovely upper gallery and – to the right of the apse, or *scarsella* – the distinctive *Tomb of the Antipope John XXIII* (1427) by Donatello and Michelozzo.

✚ *Firenze 5c* ✉ Piazza San Giovanni, Piazza del Duomo ☎ 055/230 2885 🕓 Mon–Sat 12:15–7, Sun 8:30–2. Closed Jan, Easter Sun, 24 Jun, 25–26 Dec ✋ Inexpensive 🚌 1, 6, 7, 11, 14, 23, A

CAMPANILE

The multihued Campanile is one of Italy's most beautiful bell towers, and the views from its pinnacle are a highlight of any visit to Florence. At 85m (279ft), it is just 6m (20ft) lower than the Duomo, close by, and to reach the summit you have to climb 414 steps (there is no elevator).

Begun in 1334, the tower was probably designed by Giotto, who laboured on the project during his reign as city architect and *capo maestro* (head of works). At his death in 1337, however, only the base – the first of the tower's present five levels – was complete.

Work on the second floor (1337–42) was supervised by Andrea Pisano, fresh from his work on the Baptistery's north doors. When he moved on, responsibility passed to Francesco Talenti, who completed the decoration and the remaining three floors (1348–59).

Most of the Campanile's many reliefs – probably designed by Giotto – are copies; the originals now reside in the Museo dell'Opera. Two sets decorate the first floor, the lower tier in hexagonal frames, the upper tier in diamonds. The hexagonal reliefs, by Pisano and his pupils, depict the Creation, the Arts and Industries and the Seven Sacraments. The Five Liberal Arts (Grammar, Philosophy, Music, Arithmetic and Astronomy) on the northern face are by Luca della Robbia. The upper reliefs, also the work of Pisano, portray the Seven Planets and Seven Virtues. On the second floor, the niche sculptures of the Sibyls and Prophets are copies of works by Donatello and others, now in the Museo dell'Opera.

➕ *Firenze 5c* ✉ Piazza del Duomo ☎ 055/230 2885 🕓 Daily 8:30–6:40. Closing time indicates the last admission: tower remains open 50 mins thereafter. Closed 1 Jan, Easter Sun, 8 Sep, 25–26 Dec ✋ Expensive 🚌 1, 6, 7, 11, 14, 23, A

CAPPELLA BRANCACCI

On its own, the church of Santa Maria del Carmine would merit little attention. Constructed between 1268 and 1422, it was almost completely rebuilt after a fire in 1771. One of the areas that survived, however, was the Cappella Brancacci, a tiny chapel decorated with one of the most important and influential fresco cycles in Western art. It was commissioned in 1424 by Felice Brancacci, a former Florentine ambassador to Egypt, and its decoration entrusted to Masolino da Panicale (1383–1447) and his young assistant, Tommaso di Ser Giovanni di Mone Cassai (better known by his nickname Masaccio, or 'Mad Tom'). In 1426

Masaccio's burgeoning talents were given fuller rein when Masolino was recalled to Budapest to work as a painter to the Hungarian court.

In his absence, Masaccio demonstrated a mastery of perspective, narrative drama and bold naturalism not seen in Florence since the days of Giotto. Masolino returned in 1427 but was called away to Rome a year later. Masaccio followed him after a few months, and neither painter worked in the chapel again. Masaccio died in the Holy City in 1428, at only 28 years old. In 1436 Brancacci was exiled by Cosimo de' Medici, leaving the frescoes untouched until their completion by Filippino Lippi in 1485. All but two of the frescoes depict scenes from the Life of St Peter, and all of them are outstanding, but note in particular Masaccio's powerful panel of *Adam and Eve Banished from Paradise* (top tier, extreme left). It is an excellent illustration of Masaccio's clever employment of stark and angular figures to portray profound emotion.

✚ *Firenze 1e* ✉ Santa Maria del Carmine, Piazza del Carmine ☎ Prebook by phone 055/276 8224 🕐 Mon, Wed–Sat 10–5, Sun and public hols 1–5. Closed Tue, Easter Sun, 25 Dec 💵 Moderate; combined ticket with Palazzo Vecchio expensive 🚌 D ❓ Entered via the cloisters of Santa Maria del Carmine (to the right of the church façade)

CAPPELLE MEDICEE

Best places to see, pages 36–37.

CASA BUONARROTI

The Casa Buonarroti, bought by Michelangelo in 1508, is often described as the sculptor's house (Michelangelo's surname was Buonarroti). In fact, the maestro never lived here; the present house, its decoration and its collection of Michelangelo memorabilia were arranged by his nephew Leonardo (his sole descendant), and subsequently by Leonardo's son, Michelangelo the Younger. The house, if a little impersonal, is beautifully presented, its stylish appearance the result of expensive restoration following the 1966 flood. The admission charge is a touch over-priced, however, especially given the fact that the museum contains only four minor works and a handful of drawings by the master. At the same time, the maze of decorated rooms, antique furniture, frescoed ceilings and various objets d'art are all attractive in their own right.

The sculptural highlights are on the first floor. The earliest, the *Madonna della Scala* (1491), is a delicate, shallow relief showing the influence of Donatello. Carved when Michelangelo was still in his teens, it is his earliest known work. Nearby stands the *Battle of the Centaurs* (1492), a more complex work executed when Michelangelo was employed by Lorenzo the Magnificent. The adjoining room has a wooden model of Michelangelo's plan for the façade of San Lorenzo (never realized), together with a sprawling wood-and-wax model of a torso, part of a huge river god possibly intended for the Cappelle Medicee. A room to the right contains a slender crucifix, a work believed lost until its discovery in 1965.
www.casabuonarroti.it

✚ *Firenze 7d* ✉ Via Ghibellina 70 ☎ 055/241 752 🕓 Mon, Wed–Sun 9:30–2. Closed Tue, 1 Jan, Easter Sun, 25 April, 1 May, 15 Aug, 25–26 Dec
✋ Expensive 🚌 13, 19, 23, C

DUOMO (SANTA MARIA DEL FIORE)

The first church on the site of Santa Maria del Fiore, Florence's magnificent cathedral, was built in the 7th century and dedicated to Santa Reparata, an obscure Syrian or Palestinian saint and martyr (San Lorenzo and the Baptistery served as Florence's cathedral for much of the city's early history). In the 13th century, when Florence was a prosperous and sophisticated metropolis, the city's elders declared the old church too 'crudely built and too small for such a city'. They envisaged something to rival the new cathedrals of Siena (➤ 42) and Pisa (➤ 145) – something, as an edict of 1294 put it, of the 'most exalted and most prodigal magnificence, in order that the industry and power of men may never create or undertake anything whatsoever more vast and

more beautiful'. Responsibility for designing this magnificence was entrusted to Arnolfo di Cambio in 1294. After his death, work lapsed until 1331; Giotto took over as the building's master of works in 1334. Construction of the vast Gothic nave, the tribunes (apses) and the drum and cupola of the colossal dome was finally completed in 1436.

The cathedral's interior is strikingly austere. It is also breathtaking in size – it can accommodate some 10,000 people – and ranks as Europe's fourth-largest church after St Peter's and the cathedrals of Milan and St Paul's in London. The highlights include two large frescoed equestrian portraits on the north (left) wall: one of the English mercenary Sir John Hawkwood (1436) by Paolo Uccello, the other of Niccolò da Tolentino (1456) – another soldier of fortune – by Andrea del Castagno. Note, too, the clock above the main door by Paolo Uccello and the *Tomb of Antonio d'Orso* (1323) to its right, the work of Mino da Fiesole. Much of the stained glass in the apses was designed by Lorenzo Ghiberti, as was the superb reliquary (1432–42) in the middle (third) chapel of the central apse.

The cathedral's main highlight, however, is its vast dome, one of the supreme feats of late medieval engineering. Designed by Brunelleschi, who won the commission in 1418, it was built using many innovative techniques that are still shrouded in mystery. The key to the project's success was the construction of an inner and an outer shell, as well as the use of a herringbone pattern of bricks arranged in cantilevered rings (allowing the dome to support itself as it rose). Its interior is decorated with frescoes of the *Last Judgement* (1572–9) by Vasari, much criticized over the centuries as unworthy of so great a building. They pale into insignificance alongside the view from the dome's lantern, which is reached by steps from the top of the north (left) aisle.

✚ *Firenze 5c* ✉ Piazza del Duomo ☎ 055/230 2885 🕓 Cathedral and crypt Mon–Wed, Fri 10–5, Thu 10–3:30, Sun 1:30–4:45, 1st Sat of the month 10–3:30, otherwise Sat 10–4:45. Dome: Mon–Fri 8:30–6:50, 1st Sat of month 8:30–3:20, otherwise 8:30–5. Closed Sun and public hols ✋ Cathedral: free. Dome: expensive. Crypt: inexpensive 🚌 1, 6, 7, 11, 14, 23, A

GALLERIA DEGLI UFFIZI

Best places to see, pages 44–45.

GIARDINO DI BOBOLI

Italy's most popular gardens were begun in 1549, when the Medici moved to the nearby Palazzo Pitti. They were opened to the public in 1766. Today they are one of the loveliest places in the city to rest, picnic or take a siesta. They also offer sweeping views of the Florentine skyline, notably from the belvederes (viewpoints) beside the rococo Kaffeehaus and the Giardino del Cavaliere. From the Palazzo Pitti's main courtyard, where the gardens are entered, paths lead to the Amphitheatre, a large arena designed to house Medici entertainments (it was built over the quarry used for the Palazzo's building stone). Sightseeing highlights include many antique, Renaissance and Mannerist statues; countless fountains (especially *Ganymede* and *Neptune*); and the Viottolone, a long, statue-lined avenue of cypresses that culminates in the Isolotto, a pretty, moated island garden. Free maps of the garden (in Italian text) are sometimes available on request at the ticket office.

The gardens also contain the small Museo delle Porcellane, a collection of antique porcelain, which can be visited on a combined ticket with the gardens and Museo degli Argenti (► 103).

🔡 *Firenze 4f* ✉ Piazza dei Pitti ☎ 055/23 885 🕐 Jun–Aug daily 8:15–7:30; Apr, May, Sep, Oct 9–6:30; Mar 8:15–6:30; Nov–Feb 8:15–4:30. Closed 1st and last Mon in month. Last admission 1 hour before closing. Museo delle

Porcellane: same hours as gardens 💷 Gardens: expensive. Museo delle Porcellane: expensive 🍴 Kaffeehaus (summer only) and nearby in Piazza dei Pitti (€) 🚌 11, 36, 37, D ❓ Public toilets are in the Palazzo Pitti, at the eastern side of the Amphitheatre and in the Kaffeehaus (summer only)

MUSEO DELLA CASA FIORENTINA ANTICA
(MUSEO DI PALAZZO DAVANZATI)

This beautiful medieval house offers a wonderful insight into how Florence's artists, merchants and noble families might once have lived. The house was built in about 1330 for the Davizzi, a family of

wealthy wool merchants. It was then sold to the Davanzati, who remained the owners until 1838. It opened as a museum in 1910 and was bought by the state in 1951.

In the entrance courtyard, storerooms to the rear were kept stocked in case of siege or famine, while a private well served the house with water, a luxury in an age when most water was drawn from public fountains. The wooden staircase, the only one of its kind in Florence, leads to the first of the three floors, each of which is dotted with beautifully furnished rooms and evocative medieval corners.

Highlights of the first floor include the Sala dei Pappagalli, named after the parrots *(pappagalli)* adorning its frescoes, and the gorgeous Sala Pavoni or Camera Nuziale (Wedding Room). The latter features a glorious 14th-century Sicilian bedspread, a two-winged tabernacle by Neri di Bicci and a lovely frescoed frieze of trees, peacocks *(pavoni)* and exotic birds. The third floor is given over to the delightful palace kitchen, a room often situated on the upper floor of medieval houses to minimize damage in the event of fire.

🕇 *Firenze 4d* ✉ Palazzo Davanzati, Via Porta Rossa 13 ☎ 055/238 8610
🕐 Daily 8:15–1:50. Closed 1st, 3rd, 5th Mon and 2nd, 4th Sun of month
💵 Free 🍴 In Piazza della Repubblica (€) 🚌 In the pedestrian zone: nearest services 6, 11, 31, 32, 37 to Piazza di Santa Trinità ❓ Top floor accessible only by prebooked guided tour starting at 10, 11 and 12

MUSEO BARDINI

Unjustifiably ignored by most visitors, the Museo Bardini was created by Stefano Bardini, a 19th-century art dealer whose own collection became too large for his home, and was transferred to this ersatz 'palace' created from doors, ceilings and fireplaces salvaged from demolished medieval buildings.

The exhibits are housed in some 20 rooms, which are arranged over two floors. On the ground floor, rooms 7 and 8 feature some of the museum's highlights, notably a Cosmati pulpit, a tiny carved head attributed to Nicola Pisano, and a stunning Gothic *aedicule* (canopy) framing a statue of Charity by Tino da Camaino.

The first floor begins with armour and medieval weaponry. Room 14 has two of the collection's treasures: a terracotta *Madonna and Child* and the collage-like *Madonna dei Cordai*, both attributed to Donatello. Successive rooms offer a bewitching miscellany of reliefs, furniture and majolica. Room 20 boasts two magnificently inlaid choir stalls and one of the city's grandest wooden ceilings.

✚ *Firenze 6f* ✉ Via dei Renai ☎ 055/226 4042 🕓 Sat–Mon 11–5 ✋ Moderate 🍴 On Lungarno Serristori (€) 🚌 C, D

MUSEO DI FIRENZE COM'ERA

This is one of the city's most interesting minor museums, thanks to a collection of paintings, engraving and topographical drawings evoking the

Florence of days gone by. The first room contains its principal treasure, the *Pianta della Catena*, a vast panorama of the city as it appeared in 1470. The room to its right features lunette paintings (1599) of the Medici villas by the Flemish painter van Utens – among the loveliest things in any Florentine museum.

Other highlights include the engravings of Telemaco Signorini (1874) and a vaulted room devoted to drawings and engravings of the city's major buildings.

➕ *Firenze 6c* ✉ Via dell'Oriuolo 24 ☎ 055/261 6545 🕐 Jun–Sep Mon, Tue 9–2, Sat 9–7; Oct–May Mon–Wed 9–2, Sat 9–7. Also last Sun of the month 9–2. Closed 1 Jan, Easter Sun, 1 May, 15 Aug, 25–26 Dec ✋ Inexpensive 🚌 14, 23

a walk from the Ponte Vecchio to San Miniato al Monte

This mainly uphill walk takes in some of the key sights of the Oltrarno and can easily be extended to embrace the Palazzo Pitti (➤ 102–104), Giardino di Boboli (➤ 88) and Cappella Brancacci (➤ 82–83). As a less strenuous option, it can be walked in reverse, downhill, by catching a 12 or 13 bus to Piazzale Michelangelo or San Miniato al Monte.

Cross the Ponte Vecchio and follow Via de' Guicciardini to Piazza Santa Felicita.

Santa Felicita, probably Florence's second-oldest church after San Lorenzo, is noted for Brunelleschi's Cappella Capponi, celebrated in turn for Pontormo's *Deposition* (1525–8), a masterpiece of Mannerist painting.

Take the lane left of the church and turn immediately left to Via de' Bardi. Turn right and follow Via de' Bardi. Continue to Piazza de' Mozzi if you wish to visit the

*Museo Bardini. Otherwise turn right and dog-leg up
Costa Scarpuccia. Turn left on Costa di San Giorgio.*

Number 19 Costa di San Giorgio was the home of Galileo.
At the top of the street lies Porta San Giorgio (1258), the
city's oldest-surviving gateway. To the right is the entrance
to the Forte di Belvedere (1590–95), built by Buontalenti for
Ferdinand I, with wonderful views from its ramparts.

*At Porta San Giorgio turn right and follow Via di
Belvedere and the city walls for views over olive groves
and the distant hills. At Porta San Miniato and the
crossroads at the bottom turn right. After 150m (164yds)
turn left on the stepped lane of Via di San Salvatore del
Monte. This climbs past Stations of the Cross to Viale
Galileo Galilei.*

Turn left for Piazzale Michelangelo. Turn right; after some
50m (164ft) steps and terraces lead off left to San Miniato
al Monte. The 11th-century marble-clad church is worth a
visit, and the views from here are also good if Piazzale
Michelangelo below is rather crowded.

Distance 2km (1.2 miles)
Time 45 mins or 2–3 hours with visits to churches, Museo Bardini
and Forte di Belvedere
Start point Ponte Vecchio ✚ *Firenze 4e*
End point San Miniato al Monte ✚ *Firenze 7f (off map)*
Lunch Cafés and restaurants with views on Viale Galileo Galilei

Santa Felicita
✉ Piazza Santa Felicita ☎ 055/213 018 🕒 Daily 9–12, 3–6 💶 Free

Forte di Belvedere
✉ Costa di San Giorgio–Via di Belvedere ☎ 055/262 5962 🕒 Daily
9–dusk 💶 Free except during temporary exhibitions

MUSEO NAZIONALE DEL BARGELLO
Best places to see, pages 46–47.

MUSEO DELL'OPERA DEL DUOMO
The Opera del Duomo was established in 1296 to supervise construction and maintenance of the cathedral and its many works of art. Today its sculpture collection ranks second only to the Bargello, having long housed artefacts removed for safekeeping from the Duomo, Baptistery and Campanile. The ground and mezzanine floors feature rooms filled with tools and models used during the Duomo's construction, together with sculpture removed from Arnolfo di Cambio's unfinished cathedral façade (demolished in 1587). Highlights from the latter include Donatello's *St John*, the thickset *Madonna of the Glass Eyes* and the stiff-backed figure of *Pope Boniface VIII*. Donatello insisted on having a lock put on his workshop here after a rival sculptor had sneaked in to see his work in progress. Other parts of the museum feature models (1588) for the cathedral façade (none were ever realized); several illustrated volumes of choral music; and an octagonal chapel containing reliquaries and a lovely 14th-century altarpiece (1334).

The stairs to the upper floors feature Michelangelo's outstanding *Pietà* (1550), a fitting prelude to two superlative *cantorie*, or carved choir lofts, which dominate the floor's opening room. The loft on the left (1431–8), carved in white marble, is by Luca della Robbia, that on the right (1433–9), has a far more dramatic arrangement by Donatello. The

room to the left features many age-blackened reliefs, also from the Campanile. In a room on the other side of the *cantorie* stands Donatello's extraordinary *Mary Magdalene*, while ranged around the walls are 16 statues removed from the Campanile. The museum's highlights, however, are the bronze panels crafted by Ghiberti for the Battistero doors – the focal point – paintings, mosaics and a glorious altarpiece (1459) by Antonio Pollaiuolo.

www.operaduomo.firenze.it

✚ *Firenze 6c* ✉ Piazza del Duomo 9
☎ 055/230 2885 🕓 Mon–Sat
9–7:30, Sun 9–1:45. Closed 1 Jan,
Easter Sun, 8 Sep, 25–26 Dec
♿ Expensive 🚌 1, 6, 7, 11, 14, 23, A

MUSEO DI SAN MARCO
Best places to see, pages 48–49.

MUSEO DI STORIA DELLA SCIENZA
Despite its fall from artistic grace after the Renaissance, Florence remained at the forefront of European science and learning, thanks to the work of men such as Galileo – born in nearby Pisa – and the enlightened patronage of various rulers. This well-presented and

unexpectedly fascinating museum captures the essence of the times, each of the rooms (over two floors) being devoted to a separate scientific theme or discipline.

The collection dates back to the 16th century. Cosimo I (1519–1574) kept it in the Sala delle Carte Geografiche, a map room in the Palazzo Vecchio with more than 50 painted scenes of the then known world. In 1600, Ferdinando I moved the collection to the Stazino delle Matematiche, in the Uffizi. In 1657 the Accademia del Cimento – the world's first scientific academy – began in the Palazzo Pitti. From 1829 to 1861 the workshops of the academy (which had by then moved to a different location in the city) produced some of the world's most cutting-edge scientific equipment – a sort of Silicon Valley of the 19th century – including the most accurate micrometers and telescopes. Inventor Leopoldo Nobili carried out pioneering research into electromagnetics and galvanometrics in the academy's rooms.

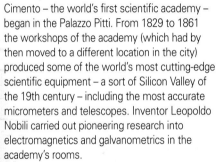

The collection moved to its current site in 1930. Highlights include a compass belonging to Michelangelo and a lens used by Galileo when he searched the skies and discovered the moons of Jupiter. A series of graphic waxworks depict the workings of the human body and a collection of old surgical instruments makes alarming yet intriguing viewing.

www.imss.fi.it

🞧 *Firenze 5e* ✉ Piazza dei Giudici 1 ☎ 055/265 311
🕐 Mon, Wed–Fri 9:30–5, Tue, Sat 9:30–1 👋 Moderate
🚌 23, B ❓ The museum is currently being renovated. During this time, temporary exhibitions taken from the permanent collection will be on show. The renovations are due to finish in early 2010

ORSANMICHELE

Orsanmichele is one of Florence's most intimate churches, providing a calm retreat from the crowds of Via dei Calzaiuoli. The earliest part of the site dates from 750, a small chapel situated in the kitchen garden *(orto)* of a Benedictine monastery. From these humble roots came its present name, which is a contraction of *San Michele ad Hortum* and *San Michele in Orto*. In 1280 the chapel was replaced with a grain market, a building destroyed by fire in 1304. In 1380 this was replaced with another church, the upper floor being retained as a granary.

Decoration of the new building was entrusted to the city's leading guilds, each of which was asked to commission a statue of its patron saint to adorn the exterior. After years of delays, statues were eventually secured from some of the greatest Renaissance artists, among them Verrocchio, Ghiberti, Donatello and Giambologna. Some of these statues, such as Donatello's *St George*, have now been replaced with copies, the originals removed for safekeeping to the church museum and other city

galleries. Others occupy their original niches and have been cleaned as part of a large ongoing restoration agenda. The interior, however, retains many of its oldest treasures, not least a magnificent glass and marble tabernacle (1348–59) by Andrea Orcagna, a work financed by votive offerings that flooded in after the Black Death of 1348. At its heart is a *Madonna and Child* (1347), a painting which is said to have inherited the miracle-working properties of a fresco on the site, destroyed in the fire of 1304. Most of the interior's frescoes, which were painted to complement the exterior sculptures, are depictions of the guild's patron saints.

✚ *Firenze 5d* ✉ Orsanmichele: Via dei Calzaiuoli (main entrance to rear on Via dell'Arte della Lana). Museum: Via dell'Arte della Lana (opposite church entrance) ☎ 055/284 944 🕐 Tue–Sun 10–5 💷 Free 🚌 In the pedestrian zone: nearest services 1, 6, 7, 11, 14, 23, A

PALAZZO MEDICI-RICCARDI

To the average bystander, this palace looks like just one more grime-covered Florentine *palazzo*. Built for Cosimo de' Medici in 1444, it was designed by Michelozzo, the Medici's leading architect, and remained the family's main home until Cosimo I moved to the Palazzo Vecchio in 1540. Its heavily rusticated ground-floor exterior, almost fortress-like in appearance, was to influence many Florentine buildings in the century of palace-building that followed. Today much of the mansion is occupied by council offices, making the survival of one of the city's most charming fresco cycles all the more remarkable.

Benozzo Gozzoli painted the three-panel *Journey of the Magi* (1459) for Piero de' Medici, probably in tribute to the Compagnia dei Magi, one of the city's leading religious confraternities (of which the Medici were key members). Tucked away in the tiny Cappella dei Magi, the cycle has been restored to stunning effect. The three principal panels deal with one of the three kings of the Nativity, though most interest derives from Gozzoli's inclusion of contemporary portraits among the sea of faces. On

the right wall, for example, the long procession is headed by a courtly figure probably intended to represent Lorenzo the Magnificent.

www.palazzo-medici.it

➕ *Firenze 5b* ✉ Via Cavour 3 ☎ 055/276 0340 🕐 Thu–Tue 9–7 ✋ Palace exterior and courtyard: free. Cappella dei Magi: expensive 🚌 1, 6, 7 ❓ Visitor numbers to Cappella dei Magi are limited. Reserve ahead

PALAZZO PITTI

Palaces and galleries do not come much larger than the Palazzo Pitti, home to the Medici for some 200 years and the setting for much of their private collection of paintings, silverware, costumes and miscellaneous objets d'art. The palace was begun in 1457 by Luca Pitti, a wealthy banker (possibly to a design by Brunelleschi), partly to upstage the Medici, then the implacable rivals of the Pittis. By 1549 the Pitti had fallen on hard times, forcing them – ironically – to sell to their old rivals. Once installed, the Medici altered the palace beyond recognition, adding two vast wings and countless additional rooms and salons.

These now house four separate museums, whose layout, ticketing and opening hours vary and can be slightly confusing. The main thing to see is the Galleria Palatina, home to a superlative collection of paintings (its entrance is to the rear right-hand side of the courtyard and up the stairs to the second floor). Within the Galleria, which is also something of a maze, you should start with the Sala di Venere, work down the following five state rooms, then return along the smaller parallel rooms to your starting point. The ceiling fresco in the Sala di Venere is the first of four, all by Piero da

Cortona, each depicting allegorical and mythological scenes inspired by the Medici. The room also contains the first of the gallery's many exceptional paintings, which here (as elsewhere) are wedged from floor to ceiling with little attempt at classification. Critics often complain at the arrangement and poor labelling, though this provides a vivid illustration of the collection's size and is how the Medici Grand Dukes chose to display their paintings.

The Sala di Apollo contains one of the gallery's many masterpieces, Titian's *Portrait of a Gentleman* (1540), along with the same artist's sensuous *Mary Magdalene* (1531) and Van Dyck's portraits of *Charles I* and *Henrietta Maria*. The next room, the Sala di Marte, features Rubens' huge *Consequences of War* (1638), an allegory of the Thirty Years' War. The next room, the Sala di Giove, was once the grand-ducal throne room. Today it is home to one of Raphael's finest portraits, the *Donna Velata* (*Veiled Woman*, 1516). More Raphaels line the walls of the next two rooms, including the famous *Madonna della Seggiola* (1515), along with works by Andrea del Sarto, Tintoretto, Giorgione, Perugino, Velázquez and others. Highlights of the parallel rooms include Crisofano Allori's celebrated *Judith and Holofernes*, Caravaggio's *Sleeping Cupid* and a sublime *Madonna and Child* by Filippo Lippi.

The most worthwhile of the Pitti's other museums is the Museo degli Argenti, whose lavish salons display the silverware, *pietra dura* vases and other priceless (if often tasteless) objects accumulated by the Medici. The Galleria d'Arte Moderna contains some 30 rooms of Tuscan paintings (1784–1945), the most interesting of which are by the *Macchiaioli* group,

often called the Italian Impressionists. The Galleria del Costume has a sumptuous collection of clothes and costumes from the heyday of the Medici court.

✚ *Firenze 3f* ✉ Piazza dei Pitti ☎ Galleria Palatina 055/238 8614. Museo degli Argenti 055/238 8709. Galleria d'Arte Moderna 056/238 8616. Galleria del Costume 055/238 8713 🕐 Galleria Palatina and Apartamenti Reali: Tue–Sun 8:15–6:50. Galleria del Costume, Museo degli Argenti and Museo delle Porcellane: hours as for Giardino di Boboli (➤ 88). Galleria d'Arte Moderna: Tue–Sun 8:15–6:50; closed 2nd, 4th Sun of month. Last ticket sold 45 mins before closing 🖐 Combined ticket for Galleria Palatina, Appartamenti Reali and Galleria d'Arte Moderna: expensive. Individual tickets for Galleria del Costume, Museo degli Argenti, Museo delle Porcellane: expensive. Combined ticket (except during major exhibitions) also includes Giardino di Boboli and Museo Barolini 🍴 Piazza dei Pitti (€) 🚌 36, 37, D ❓ Hours for the minor museums can change constantly according to the time of year, check with the tourist office

PALAZZO VECCHIO

The Palazzo Vecchio, designed by Arnolfo di Cambio, then also employed on the Duomo, was finished in 1303, but radically altered by Cosimo I in 1540 when he moved the Medici court here from the Palazzo Medici-Riccardi. When Cosimo moved again in 1550, this time to the 'new' Palazzo Pitti, the palace took its present name (*vecchio* means 'old').

Its courtyard (1453) was designed by Michelozzo, one of the Medici's preferred architects, and later adorned by Vasari with decorative panels. Vasari also built the staircase that leads to the palace's focal point, the vast but soulless Salone dei Cinquecento, built in 1495 to accommodate the 500 members of Florence's ruling assembly. Vasari decorated both its ceiling – whose gilt-laden paintings glorify Cosimo I – and the walls, whose six huge paintings (1563–5) depict a succession of Florentine military triumphs. Beneath them may be a series of unfinished frescoes

begun in 1503–4 by Michelangelo and Leonardo. A statue of *Victory* (1525) by Michelangelo stands almost opposite the Salone's entrance, while just off the chamber is the Studiolo (entrance door wall), a tiny but exquisitely decorated room. On the second floor enjoy the view from the Terrazza di Saturno, the many decorated rooms – notably Bronzino's Mannerist chapel – and the view of the Piazza della Signoria from the Sala d'Udienza. The Sala dei Gigli has frescoes by Domenico Ghirlandaio and Donatello's statue of *Judith and Holofernes*. Kids will enjoy the interactive workshops at the palace's innovative Museo dei Ragazzi (Children's Museum).

✚ *Firenze 5e* ✉ Piazza della Signoria ☎ 055/276 8224 ⏱ Fri–Wed 9–7, Thu 9–2; last admission 1 hour before closing. Closed 1 Jan, Easter Sun, 1 May, 15 Aug, 25–26 Dec ✋ Expensive (includes entry to Cappella Brancacci) 🚌 In the pedestrian zone: nearest services 19, 23, 31, 32, A ❓ Hour-long tours (Mon–Sat; includes admission to palace) take visitors to parts of the palace normally closed: reserve in advance at ticket office

PIAZZA DELLA SIGNORIA

While the Piazza del Duomo was Florence's religious focus, the Piazza della Signoria has long served as the city's civic and political heart. Witness to countless momentous events across the centuries, such as the burning of Savonarola in 1498, it remains one of the city's busiest meeting places and the natural conclusion of the evening *passeggiata* (stroll) along Via dei Calzaiuoli. It was first enlarged at the start of the 14th century to accommodate the Palazzo dei Priori (now the Palazzo Vecchio), and was paved as early as 1385.

Sights include the Palazzo Vecchio; the Uffizi (off the square to the south); and the Loggia dei Lanzi, an outdoor gallery sheltering several outstanding pieces of sculpture. Greatest of these are Cellini's *Perseus* (1554) and Giambologna's contorted *Rape of the Sabine Women* (1583), though there are plans to replace these and other of the loggia's sculptures with copies.

More statues adorn the piazza itself. From left to right as you face the Palazzo Vecchio they include Giambologna's equestrian statue of Cosimo I (1587–94); the Neptune Fountain (1563–75) by Ammananti; next the *Marzocco*, a copy of Donatello's Florentine heraldic lion; *Judith and Holofernes* (1456–60), a copy of Donatello's statue in the Palazzo Vecchio; *David*, an 1873 copy of Michelangelo's most famous sculpture; and Bandinelli's *Hercules and Cacus* (1534), a work intended to symbolize Cosimo I, Florentine fortitude and the defeat of domestic enemies. On its unveiling the work was described by a fellow sculptor as a 'sack of melons'.

✚ *Firenze 5d* ✉ Piazza della Signoria ☎ None ⏱ Daily, 24 hours 💷 Free 🍴 Rivoire (Piazza della Signoria 5r; €€) 🚍 In the pedestrian zone: nearest services 19, 23, 31, 32, A

PONTE VECCHIO

The Ponte Vecchio and its huddle of old buildings are among the most familiar sights of Florence. Pitched close to the Arno's narrowest point, this is the last in a long succession of bridges on the site, dating back to Roman times. In 1944 it was the only Florentine bridge spared by the retreating Nazis, reputedly saved on Hitler's direct orders. In 1966 it was spared again – just – when it withstood the flood that brought death and destruction to much of Florence.

Until 1218 the bridge was the city's only river crossing, providing a vital lifeline between the old heart and the Oltrarno, on the Arno's southern bank. The present structure, which dates from 1345, was built to replace a bridge swept away in the floods of 1333 (some of the worst in the city's history). Its name ('Old Bridge') was coined

to distinguish it from the Arno's other bridge, the Ponte alla Carraia, originally built in 1218.

Shops first appeared on the bridge during the 14th century, most of them butchers and fishmongers. The next arrivals were the tanners, who soaked hides in the river before adding to the communal stench by tanning them with horse's urine. Across the top of the shops runs the Corridoio Vasariano, built by Vasari to enable Cosimo I to walk undisturbed between his home (the Palazzo Vecchio) and offices (the Uffizi). In 1593 Ferdinand I raised shop rents and decreed that only jewellers and goldsmiths should occupy the bridge. They remain to this day.

✚ *Firenze 4e* ✉ Ponte Vecchio ☎ None ⏰ Daily, 24 hours ♿ Free 🚌 B, D
❓ Corridoio Vasariano occasionally open to visitors: consult Uffizi or tourist office for current opening times

SANTISSIMA ANNUNZIATA

The church of Santissima Annunziata lies on one of Florence's lesser-known but most architecturally pleasing squares. Laid out by Brunelleschi in the 1420s, the area was altered several times over the next 200 years, the most notable additions being an equestrian statue of Ferdinand I (1608) by Giambologna and two bizarre little fountains, the work of Giambologna's pupil, Pietro Tacca.

The church was built to praise the Annunciation, a crucial event in the life of the city: In the old Florentine calendar, the New Year began on the Feast of the Annunciation (25 March). It is now the mother church of the Servites, an order founded in 1234 by would-be servants *(servi)* of the Virgin.

The order built a chapel, which began drawing the crowds after 1252, when a painting begun by a Servite monk was miraculously completed by an angel. By 1450 so many pilgrims were coming that a new church, paid for by the Medici, was commissioned to house the painting. Via dei Servi was built at the same time to link

SS Annunziata and the Duomo, the two most important churches in the city dedicated to the Virgin.

The church's main sight is the inner courtyard, the Chiostro dei Voti (1447), swathed in frescoes by Andrea del Sarto, Jacopo Pontormo and Rosso Fiorentino. Inside the main body of the church lies Michelozzo's magnificent Tempietto (1448–61), built to shelter the miraculous painting. The first two chapels on the left feature celebrated works by Andrea del Castagno.

🏛 *Firenze 7a* ✉ Piazza della Santissima Annunziata ☎ 055/266 181 🕐 Daily 7:30–12:30, 4–6:30 ✋ Free 🚌 6, 31, 32, C ❓ The eastern side of Piazza della Santissima Annunziata is dominated by a loggia (1493) built by Brunelleschi for the Ospedale degli Innocenti, whose small Renaissance art collection and contrasting 'Men's' and 'Women's' cloisters are open to the public

Ospedale degli Innocenti

✉ Piazza della Santissima Annunziata 12 ☎ 055/203 7308 🕐 Mon–Sat 8:30–7, Sun 8:30–2. Closed 1 Jan, Easter Sun, 1 May, 15 Aug, 25–26 Dec ✋ Moderate

SANT'APOLLONIA

Much of the former Benedictine convent of Sant'Apollonia has been converted into apartments, but the former refectory – the first Renaissance convent refectory in the city (1445) – features an entire wall frescoed with *The Last Supper* (1450), or *Cenacolo* in Italian, a subject that was often depicted in monastic and other religious eating places for obvious reasons. The work of Andrea del Castagno, it was uncovered in the 19th century, having been painted over by the nuns. It is an unsettling masterpiece, full of blood-red tones and featuring a devilish and black-bearded Judas.

🏛 *Firenze 5a* ✉ Via XXVII Aprile 1 ☎ 055/238 8607 🕐 Tue–Sat, 2nd, 4th Sun and 1st, 3rd, 5th Mon of month 8:15–1:50. Ticket office closes 30 mins earlier ✋ Free 🚌 1, 6, 7, 10, 11, C and other services to Piazza San Marco

SANTA CROCE

Best places to see, pages 52–53.

SAN LORENZO

San Lorenzo was founded in 393, making it one of the oldest churches in Florence. It served as the city's cathedral until the 7th century. A Romanesque church built on the site in 1060 survived until 1419, when Giovanni de' Medici and a group of parishioners offered to pay for a new church. Brunelleschi, then working on the Duomo, started work two years later, but progress faltered in the face of political and financial upheavals and only resumed when Giovanni's son, Cosimo de' Medici, offered 40,000 florins to ensure its completion (150 florins at this time could support a family for a year). As a result, the church became the Medici's dynastic church, while its rear portion, the Cappelle Medicee, became their private chapel (▶ 36–37).

The interior is an early Renaissance masterpiece. Brunelleschi created 'sails' of creamy wall interspersed with austere grey *pietra serena*. Artistic highlights include Rosso Fiorentino's *Marriage of the Virgin* (second altar on the right) and Desiderio da Settignano's *Pala del Sacramento* (1451–68), on the wall at the end of the right nave.

In the middle of the church stand two raised pulpits (1455–66), among the last works of Donatello (and pupils), and in front of the high altar brass grilles mark the tomb of Cosimo de' Medici (with a plaque inscribed *Pater Patriae* – Father of the Fatherland). The *Martyrdom of St Laurence* (1565–9), left of the two pulpits, is a graphic painting by Bronzino. In a chapel around the corner is a cenotaph (monument) to Donatello, who died in 1466 and was buried near Cosimo, his friend and patron. Brunelleschi's Sagrestia Vecchia, or Old Sacristy (1421), a simple architectural gem, is entered from the left transept of the church. On the left as you enter stands the bronze and porphyry tomb of Giovanni and Piero de' Medici (Cosimo de' Medici's sons), and in the middle is the tomb of Giovanni and Piccarda, Cosimo's parents and founders of the Medici fortune.

Most of the sacristy's decoration (1434–43) is by Donatello, most notably the eight tondi showing the Evangelists and scenes from the life of St John (Giovanni's patron saint). The reliefs above the doors of the end wall portray Cosmos and Damian, the Medici's patron saints, and saints Laurence and Stephen, protectors of Florence.

From the church cloisters, stairs lead to the Biblioteca Laurenziana, begun in 1524 to house the Medici's vast 100-year-old library, collected by agents sent as far afield as Germany and the Middle East. Michelangelo designed the Ricetto (Vestibule), with its revolutionary use of space, and almost every detail of the

library Reading Room – even the desks. The four rooms beyond contain a fraction of the books and manuscripts.

🔲 *Firenze 4b* ✉ Piazza San Lorenzo 🚌 In the pedestrian zone

San Lorenzo ☎ 055/214 042 🕐 Mon–Fri 10–5:30, Sat, Sun 1:30–5:30. Closed Sun Nov–Feb 🖐 Moderate

Biblioteca Laurenziana ☎ 055/214 443 or 210 760; www.bml.firenze.sbn.it 🕐 Open to the public only during exhibitions 🖐 Exhibitions inexpensive

SANTA MARIA NOVELLA

Santa Maria Novella ranks second only to Santa Croce in the pantheon of great Florentine churches. Begun as a simple chapel in the 9th century, it was rebuilt in 1094 and christened Santa Maria delle Vigne (Mary of the Vineyards). It then passed to the Dominicans, who in 1246 began a new church. The Romanesque façade was not finished until 1456, when Leon Battista Alberti completed the multihued frontage.

The lofty Gothic interior has several important frescoes, the most famous of which is Masaccio's *Trinità* (1428), midway down the left wall, one of the first Renaissance paintings to put the new theories of perspective to good use. Close by is Brunelleschi's pulpit (1443–52), where the Inquisition first denounced Galileo for agreeing with Copernicus that the earth revolved around the sun.

Many of the church's chapels were commissioned by leading Renaissance businessmen. Banker Filippo Strozzi employed Filippino Lippi to fresco the Cappella di Filippo Strozzi with scenes from the life of his namesake, St Philip (Filippo) the Apostle. The chapel to its right, the Cappella Bardi, features faded 14th-century frescoes, some attributed to Cimabue, Giotto's first teacher.

To the left of the Strozzi chapel, in the chancel, is Domenico Ghirlandaio's beautiful fresco cycle on the *Life of the Virgin* (left wall) and *Life of St John the Baptist* (right wall). Despite their religious themes, these are actually vignettes of daily life in 15th-century Florence; they were commissioned by another banker, Giovanni Tornabuoni, whose relations appear in several scenes.

More frescoes (1351–7), the work of Nardo di Cione, adorn the Cappella Strozzi (up steps at the top left-hand side of the church): *Paradiso* (left wall); the *Last Judgement* (behind the altar) and a map-like *Inferno* (right wall). The altarpiece is by Nardo's brother, Andrea di Cione, better known as Orcagna, and shows *Christ Giving the Keys to St Peter and the Book of Knowledge to Thomas Aquinas* (the chapel is dedicated to Aquinas).

Left of Santa Maria's façade is the entrance to the church museum and Chiostro Verde (Green Cloister), named after the green pigment of its badly faded frescoes. Despite the

deterioration, many of the panels are superb – especially Paolo Uccello's *Universal Deluge* (1430), whose lurching composition illustrates his obsession with perspective. Notice the arks to either side of the picture, depicted before and after the Flood.

Off the cloister lies the Cappellone degli Spagnoli, once used by the Spanish entourage of Eleanor of Toledo, wife of Cosimo I. It features one of the city's most striking fresco cycles, the work of Andrea da Firenze.

The left wall shows *The Triumph of Doctrine,* with Thomas Aquinas enthroned amid the Virtues and Doctors of the Church.

The right wall portrays *The Work and Triumph of the Dominican Order*, with St Dominic unleashing the 'hounds of the Lord' (*Domini canes*, a pun on 'Dominicans'). The four women are the Four Vices, surrounded by dancing and other debaucheries. A nearby friar hears confessions before sending the saved heavenwards; above the kneeling pilgrims are portraits of Dante, Petrarch, Giotto and others.

✚ *Firenze 3b* ✉ Piazza Santa Maria Novella ☎ Santa Maria Novella: 055/219 257. Museo di Santa Maria Novella: 055/282 187 🕐 Santa Maria Novella: Mon–Thu 9–5, Fri 1–5, Sat 9–5, Sun 1–5. Museo di Santa Maria Novella: Mon–Thu, Sat 9–5. Closed Fri, Sun and 1 Jan, Easter Sun, 25 Apr, 1 May, 15 Aug, 25, 26 Dec ✋ Santa Maria Novella: free. Museo di Santa Maria Novella: inexpensive ⌂ In Piazza Santa Maria Novella (€) 🚌 All services to the rail station ❓ Guided tours of the church occasionally available

SAN MINIATO AL MONTE

The most beautiful church in Florence takes its name from St Minias, a Greek or Armenian Christian merchant who was martyred in Florence in AD250. According to legend the saint picked up his severed head and carried it from his place of execution (close to Piazza della Signoria) across the Arno to the hilltop site where his church now stands. Most of the present building dates from 1013, making it among the city's oldest churches.

The Romanesque façade (1090–1270) features a mosaic of Christ, Mary and St Minias (1260) and a gilded eagle clasping a bale of wool – symbol of the Arte di Calimala, the wealthy guild that was made responsible for the church's fabric in 1228.

The breathtaking interior is dominated by a sumptuous painted wooden ceiling (1322) and a famous inlaid floor (1207), reputedly inspired by Sicilian fabrics, and patterned with lions, doves and the signs of the zodiac. The capitals on the pillars of the nave are Roman and Byzantine originals. In the left-hand aisle is the Cappella del Cardinale del Portogallo, a Renaissance masterpiece complete with paintings, glazed terracotta and funerary sculpture, the works of sculptor Antonio Rossellino and painters Baldovinetti and two brothers Antonio and Pietro Pollaiuolo. The Cardinal of

Portugal, whose uncle was King of Portugal, died in Florence in 1459 and was buried here. At the end of the nave, alongside Michelozzo's free-standing Cappella del Crocifisso (1448), steps lead to the raised choir and a magnificent carved pulpit and screen (1207). The sacristy, off to the right, boasts a vivid fresco cycle by Spinello Aretino depicting *Scenes from the Life of St Benedict* (1387).

✝ *Firenze 7f (off map)* ✉ Off Viale Galileo Galilei ☎ 055/234 2731
🕐 Summer daily 8–7; winter Mon–Sat 8–12, 3–6, Sun 3–6 ✋ Free
🍴 In Viale Galileo Galilei (€–€€) 🚌 12, 13

SANTA TRINITÀ

Santa Trinità is something of an architectural curiosity. Its flamboyant baroque exterior makes a striking contrast with the

calm, Gothic assurance of its interior. Founded in 1092, it was rebuilt between 1258 and 1280 – possibly to a design by Nicola Pisano – and the façade was added by Buontalenti in 1593.

The dusky, atmospheric interior has several wonderful works of art, most notably Domenico Ghirlandaio's frescoes (1483) in the Cappella Sassetti (the right-hand chapel to the right of the high altar). They represent

episodes from the life of St Francis and were commissioned by
Francesco Sassetti in a bid to outdo his rival, Francesco Tornabuoni,
who had paid for the frescoes in Santa Maria Novella, also by
Ghirlandaio.

The panel portraying *St Francis Receiving the Rule* in the lunette
above the altar is famous for its setting – the Piazza della Signoria
– and its portraits, which include Sassetti, who worked for the
Medici bank, between his son, Federigo, and Lorenzo the
Magnificent. On the stairs stand the humanist Poliziano and three
of his pupils, the sons of Lorenzo the Magnificent.

The chapel's altarpiece, also by Ghirlandaio (1485), depicts *The
Adoration of the Magi,* combining classical and Christian motifs
(notice the Roman sarcophagus). Sassetti and his wife are
portrayed to either side. Other works of art include Lorenzo
Monaco's early 15th-century frescoes (fourth chapel on the right),
the *Tomb of Bishop Federighi* (1454–7) by Luca della Robbia
(second chapel left of the altar) and frescoes by Neri di Bicci and
Bicci di Lorenzo (fourth chapel on the left).

🌼 *Firenze 3d* ✉ Piazza di Santa Trinità ☎ 055/216 912 🕒 Mon–Sat 8–12,
4–6, Sun 4–6. Summer hours may be longer 👆 Free 🚌 6, 11, 31, 32, 36, 37, B

HOTELS

Annalena (€)

A popular pension-style hotel in an old Medici palace opposite the Boboli gardens. Some rooms have terraces and garden views.

✉ Via Romana 34 ☎ 055/222 402; www.hotelannalena.it 🚌 11, 36

Beacci Tornabuoni (€€–€€€)

A venerable hotel converted from a 14th-century *palazzo* on Florence's premier shopping street. The rooms are elegantly faded, some smaller and less well furnished than others.

✉ Via dei Tornabuoni 3 ☎ 055/212 645 or 268 377; www.tornabuonihotels.com 🚌 6, 11, 36, 37, A

Brunelleschi (€€€)

A conversion around a fine medieval tower in a quiet position just behind Via dei Calzaiuoli. An excellent, central hotel.

✉ Piazza Sant'Elisabetta 3 ☎ 055/27370; www.hotelbrunelleschi.it 🚌 In the pedestrian zone: nearest services 1, 6, 7, 11, 14

Casci (€–€€)

A good, family-run budget hotel just off the Piazza dell Duomo. Rooms are simple but clean and the location is great.

✉ Via Cavour 13 ☎ 055/211 686; www.hotelcasci.com 🚌 1, 6, 7, 10, 11, 17

Helvetia & Bristol (€€€)

Restoration has made this Florence's finest luxury hotel. A central position between Via dei Tornabuoni and Piazza della Repubblica makes it an ideal base for shopping and sightseeing.

✉ Via dei Pescioni 2 ☎ 055/26651; www.royaldemeure.com 🚌 6, 11, 36, 37

Hermitage (€€)

A very well-known hotel overlooking the Ponte Vecchio; popular with UK and US visitors. The windows of the rooms at the front are double-glazed; the rooms at the back are quieter. There's a welcoming, family-run atmosphere.

✉ Vicolo Marzio 1, off Piazza del Pesce ☎ 055/287 216; www.hermitagehotel.com 🚌 B

J & J (€€)

A quiet, small and intimate hotel in a former 16th-century monastery with tasteful rooms, east of the main hub.

✉ Via di Mezzo 20 ☎ 055/263 121; www.jandj.hotelinfirenze.com 🚌 B
❓ Has a loyal group of clients, so reserve well ahead

Loggiato dei Serviti (€€–€€€)

A conversion in the vaulted interior of the 16th-century former Servites' monastery, with calm and airy rooms.

✉ Piazza Santissima Annunziata 3 ☎ 055/289 592;
www.loggiatodeiservitihotel.it 🚌 6, 31, 32 ❓ Advance reservations essential

Morandi alla Crocetta (€€–€€€)

A small, welcoming 10-room hotel that is part of a former 16th-century monastery just east of Piazza Santissima Annunziata.

✉ Via Laura 50 ☎ 055/234 4747; www.hotelmorandi.it 🚌 1, 6, 7, 10, 11, 17

Porta Faenza (€€)

One of the better hotels close to the station and San Lorenzo market area. Spacious rooms with modern fittings.

✉ Via Faenza 77 ☎ 055/284 119; www.hotelportafaenza.it 🚌 All services to Santa Maria Novella rail station

Residenza (€–€€)

Acceptable if rather unexciting rooms on the top floors of a 17th-century *palazzo*. Good value, given the excellent location, though rooms looking onto the street can be noisy.

✉ Via dei Tornabuoni 8 ☎ 055/218 684; www.laresidenzahotel.com
🚌 6, 11, 36, 37, A

Scaletta (€–€€)

Scaletta is on the top floor of a 15th-century palace and is usually remarkably peaceful given the Oltrarno location. There are spacious and simply furnished rooms, together with two excellent terraces with views looking towards the Palazzo Pitti and Giardino di Boboli.

✉ Via Guicciardini 13 ☎ 055/283 028; www.hotellascaletta.it 🚌 11, 37, D

Westin Excelsior (€€€)

The better of the two famous, grand old hotels on this rather lack-lustre square by the river. The rooms are old-world in look and feel, and most have more character than those of the *Grand* opposite.

✉ Piazza Ognissanti 3 ☎ 055/27151; www.westin.com 🚌 11, 17, B

RESTAURANTS

FLORENCE EAST
Alle Murate (€€)

Among the city's top-rated restaurants. The cooking is simple, revelling in innovative interpretations of traditional Tuscan and southern Italian dishes. The historic vaulted dining room is decorated with beautiful frescoes.

✉ Via del Proconsolo 16r ☎ 055/240 618 🕐 Reserve ahead. Closed lunch, Mon and Aug 🚌 14, 23, A

Baldovino (€€)

See page 58.

Cibreo (€€)

See page 59.

Da Ganino (€–€€)

See page 59.

Dino (€€)

Dino is one of the city's most venerable restaurants and over the years has served consistently good Tuscan food to generations of Florentines. Suitable for family outings and business lunches alike.

✉ Via Ghibellina 47r ☎ 055/241 452 🕐 Closed Sun evening and Mon lunch 🚌 A

Enoteca Pinchiorri (€€€)

There is no question that this is one of Florence's best (and most expensive) restaurants. Its lovely 15th-century *palazzo* setting, food and wine cellar are without rival, though the rarified atmosphere and ceremony associated with eating here may not

be to all tastes. Jacket and tie recommended for men.
✉ Via Ghibellina 87 ☎ 055/242 777; www.enotecapinchiorri.com
🕐 Reservations essential. Closed Sun–Tue and lunch Wed, also Aug and
Christmas 🚌 13, 23, A

Osteria del Caffé Italiano (€€–€€€)

A combination of wine bar, trattoria and *ristorante*. The building
used to be a *palazzo*, so the décor is historic Tuscan.
✉ Via Isole delle Stinche ☎ 055/289 368; www.caffeitaliano.it
🕐 Tue–Sun noon–1am 🚌 14

Paoli (€€)

The food here may not be the best in the city, but few Florentine
restaurants are as old or as beautiful. Most people come here for
the atmospheric vaulted and frescoed dining room. The location
is also very central (take the street off Via dei Calzaiuoli opposite
Orsanmichele). Reserve or arrive early to be sure of getting a seat.
✉ Via dei Tavolini 12r ☎ 055/216 215; www.casatrattoria.com
🕐 Closed Tue 🚌 In the pedestrian zone: nearest services 1, 6, 7, 11, 14, A

FLORENCE NORTH

Antellesi (€–€€)

See page 58.

Don Chisciotte (€€)

Smaller than many Florentine restaurants and with three high-
vaulted and tastefully appointed dining rooms. Much – but not all –
of Don Chisciotte's menu is devoted to fish, together with some
interesting seafood and pasta combinations. On a street off the
west side of Piazza dell'Indipendenza (northeast of the station).
✉ Via Cosimo Ridolfi 4r ☎ 055/475 430; www.ristorantedonchisciotte.it
🕐 Closed Mon lunch, Sun and Aug 🚌 All services to the rail station

Le Fonticine (€€)

This well-known family-run restaurant combines dishes from
Tuscany and Emilia-Romagna. The rustic atmosphere suggests
it has tourists in mind, but the traditional food, especially the

home-made pastas, is perfectly acceptable. Try the wild boar *(cinghiale)* and tripe *(trippa)* if you are feeling adventurous.
✉ Via Nazionale 79r ☎ 055/282 106; www.lefonticine.com ⊘ Closed Sun, Mon and three weeks in Aug 🚌 Services to the rail station

Sabatini (€€€)
This stylish and historic restaurant was formerly one of Florence's most exalted dining places. The Italian-International food is now only intermittently outstanding, though it still remains good enough to satisfy more than its fair share of Florentines. Service and the choice of wines are both generally excellent.
✉ Via Panzani 9a ☎ 055/282 802; www.ristorantesabatini.it ⊘ Closed Mon 🚌 14, 17, 23, A

Taverna del Bronzino (€€)
The cooking is traditional Tuscan, the service efficient and courteous. Pastas are good, especially the *linguine al pesto* and *cappellacci al cedro*. Both meat and fish dishes are available.
✉ Via delle Ruote 25r ☎ 055/495 220 ⊘ Closed Sun and Aug 🚌 6, 7, 11 and other services to San Marco

FLORENCE WEST
Belle Donne (€–€€)
See page 59.

Cantinetta Antinori (€€€€)
See page 59.

Latini (€)
See page 59.

Zà-Zà (€–€€)
Zà-Zà has been serving the central market's traders and customers for more than 20 years, offering set-price meals in an inviting brick-arched and stone-walled interior. It has become better known, thanks to some high-profile celebrity customers, and prices have crept up. Reserve in summer.

✉ Piazza del Mercato Centrale 26r ☎ 055/215 411; www.trattoriazaza.it
🕐 Closed Sun and part of Aug 🚌 On the edge of the pedestrian zone

FLORENCE OLTRARNO
Angiolino (€–€€)
Food here can be slightly erratic, but this is a pretty and also reasonably priced restaurant that remains true to its Florentine culinary roots. The varied *antipasti* are particularly good.
✉ Via Santo Spirito 36r ☎ 055/239 8976 🕐 Closed late Jul to mid-Aug
🚌 D stops one block away

Osteria del Cinghiale Bianco (€)
A great place to enjoy delicious Tuscan staples, including *ribollita* (bean soup) and tender *cinghiale* (wild boar), after which the restaurant is named. The owners give a warm welcome.
✉ Borgo S Jacopo 43r ☎ 055/215 706; www.cinghialebianco.it
🕐 Mon, Tue, Thu, Fri 6:30pm–10:30pm, Sat, Sun 12–3, 6:30–10:30
🚌 D

Quattro Leoni (€–€€)
A welcoming, informal place in three airy wood-beamed rooms with modern paintings on the medieval stone walls. The food consists of unfussy Florentine standards leavened with the odd twist of culinary invention. Tucked away in a small piazza.
✉ Via del Vellutini 1r–Piazza della Passera ☎ 055/218 562;
www.4leoni.com 🕐 Closed Wed lunch 🚌 36, 37

SHOPPING

BOOKS, MAPS AND GUIDES
Feltrinelli
An excellent central bookshop with plenty of foreign titles.
✉ Via Cavour 12–20r ☎ 055/219 524; www.lafeltrinelli.it 🚌 6, 17, 23

Libreria Le Monnier
For years this has been one of the most professional bookshops in the city. Italian and international titles. Cultured and helpful staff.
✉ Via San Gallo 53r, one block west of Via Cavour ☎ 055/483 215 🚌 1, 6, 7

FASHION

There are many designer stores on and around Via dei Tornabuoni and the nearby Via della Vigna Nuova. These include:

Armani

✉ Via dei Tornabuoni 48r ☎ 055/219 041; www.armani.com

Emilio Pucci

✉ Via dei Tornabuoni 20–22r ☎ 055/265 8082; www.emiliopucci.com

✉ Palazzo Pucci, Via de' Pucci 6 ☎ 055/261 841

Emporio Armani

✉ Piazza Strozzi 16r ☎ 055/284 315; www.emporioarmani.com

Dolce e Gabbana

✉ Via degli Strozzi 12–18r ☎ 055/281 003; www.dolcegabbana.com

Gucci

✉ Via dei Tornabuoni 73r ☎ 055/264 011; www.gucci.com

Max Mara

✉ Via dei Pecori 23r ☎ 055/287 761

✉ Max & Co, Via dei Calzaiuoli 89r ☎ 055/288 656; www.maxandco.com

Prada

✉ Via dei Tornabuoni 67r ☎ 055/283 439; www.prada.com

Valentino

✉ Via dei Tosinghi 52r ☎ 055/293 142; www.valentino.com

FOOD AND WINE

Casa del Vino

Spend time at this wine bar tasting the local labels and buying bottles of the ones you like to take home.

✉ Via dell'Ariento 16r ☎ 055/215 609; www.casadelvino.it 🚌 4, 12, 25, 31, 32, 33 to Via Nazionale

Pegna

See page 64.

Stenio

This small family-owned shop sells local wines and olive oils, plus cheeses and sandwiches. It's close to the Mercato Centrale.

✉ Via Sant' Antonino 49r ☎ 055/216 889 🚌 4, 12, 25, 31, 32, 33 to Via Nazionale

JEWELLERY
Caputi

Caputi is one of the most famous names in top-class Italian costume jewellery. There's another branch at Borgo Santi Apostoli 44–46r.

✉ Via Santo Spirito 58r ☎ 055/212 972; www.angelacaputi.com 🚌 D stops one block away

Fratelli Piccini

Family jewellers since 1880, with a shop on goldsmith's row on the Ponte Vecchio, this company produces modern pieces using precious and semi-precious stones.

✉ Ponte Vecchio 23r ☎ 055/294 768; www.fratellipiccini.com
🚌 In the pedestrian zone

Parenti

Florentines in search of the perfect gift often make a beeline for this lovely and legendary shop. Silverware, porcelain, glass, ceramics, candles and jewellery.

✉ Via dei Tornabuoni 93r ☎ 055/214 438 🚌 6, 11, A

Torrini

Jacopo Torrini patented his mark in 1369. Six centuries later one of his descendants still runs this distinguished jewellers.

✉ Piazza del Duomo 10r ☎ 055/230 2401; www.torrini.com 🚌 A (in the pedestrian zone)

Vincenti

One of the many historic shops on the Ponte Vecchio (see also Fratelli Piccini, above), this jewellery store has been here since the 16th century.

✉ Ponte Vecchio 16r ☎ 055/291 065; www.vincentigioielli.it 🚌 B, D (in the pedestrian zone)

LEATHER GOODS
Cellerini

See page 64.

Raspini
This designer name is a byword among Florentines for high-quality shoes, belts and other leather and fashion goods.
✉ Via Por Santa Maria 72r. Also Via Roma 25r and Via Martinelli 1–5r
☎ 055/215 796; www.raspini.com 🚍 In the pedestrian zone north of the Ponte Vecchio

PAPER AND STATIONERY
Il Papiro
See page 64.

Parione
This shop is a superb source of paper, pens, marbled paper and leather-bound books.
✉ Via del Parione 10r, off Piazza Santa Trinità ☎ 055/215 684 🚍 6 or 11 to Piazza Santa Trinità–Via dei Tornabuoni; also A, B

Pineider
See page 64.

Il Torchio
First-rate traditional Florentine marbled paper is available at this store. You can choose from a selection of small paper-covered goods or buy sheets of paper.
✉ Via dei Bardi 17 ☎ 055/234 2862; www.legatoriailtorchio.com
🚍 C, D

PRINTS
Giovanni Baccani
See page 64–65.

SHOES
Beltrami
A well-known nationwide chain which sells not only shoes but a small selection of jackets.
✉ Via della Vigna Nuova 70r ☎ 055/287 779; www.beltramifirenze.it 🚍 6, 11, A

Fratelli Rossetti
Another country-wide chain for expensive high-quality shoes.
✉ Piazza della Repubblica 43–5r ☎ 055/216 656 🚇 A

Salvatore Ferragamo
See page 65.

ENTERTAINMENT

Listings of current and forthcoming events can be obtained from the tourist office; from newspapers such as *La Nazione* and *La Repubblica*; and from listings magazines such as *Metro* and *Firenze Spettacolo* (www.firenzespettacolo.it).

CLASSICAL MUSIC
Florence's main classical music events take place during its big summer festivals. During the rest of the year numerous smaller recitals of music are held in the city's churches and concert halls.

Amici della Musica
This group organizes an October to April season of Saturday afternoon concerts (usually at Teatro della Pergola).
Box office: ✉ Via Alammani 39 ☎ 055/210 804
Information: ☎ 055/607 440; www.amicimusica.fi.it
Teatro della Pergola: ✉ Via della Pergola 18 ☎ 055/226 4333, 055/226 4316

Musicus Concentus
Musicus Concentus holds recitals between October and June at various locations, including the Palazzo dei Congressi.
Box office: ✉ Piazza del Carmine 19 ☎ 055/210 804. Information: 055/287 347; www.musicusconcentus.com

Orchestera Regionale
Presents concerts in churches such as Santo Stefano.
✉ Via delle Pesce (off Via Por Santa Maria) or Teatro Verdi ☎ 055/234 0710

Palazzo dei Congressi
✉ Viale F Strozzi (north of the rail station) ☎ No phone

Teatro Comunale

The city's key performance venue runs its own season of smaller concerts (Sep to mid-Dec), together with opera performances (Dec–Jan) and occasional symphony concerts (Jan–Apr). The neighbouring (and contemporary) Teatro del Maggio Musicale Fiorentino also hosts many performances throughout the year.

✉ Corso Italia 16, off Lungarno Amerigo Vespucci ☎ 055/277 9350; www.maggiofiorentino.com 🚌 B

Teatro Puccini

Hosts a variety of performances, including opera.

✉ Via delle Cascine 41 ☎ 055/362 067; www.teatropuccini.it 🚌 17, 176

Teatro Verdi

The slightly smaller Teatro Verdi mixes opera and ballet productions with its theatrical repertoire between January and April.

✉ Via Ghibellina 99 ☎ 055/212 320; www.teatroverdifirenze.it 🚌 14, A

NIGHTLIFE

Andromeda

A popular and very central club-disco.

✉ Via dei Cimatori 13–Piazza dei Cerchi 7a ☎ 055/292 002 🕐 Closed Sun 🚌 A (in the pedestrian zone)

Auditorium Flog

The city's best-known venue for live rock and jazz concerts.

✉ Via Mercanti 24b ☎ 055/477 978; www.flog.it 🚌 4, B

Full Up

This place has been around for some time and is especially popular with a slightly older, more refined crowd at the weekends.

✉ Via della Vigna Vecchia 21, off Via del Proconsolo ☎ 055/293 006; www.fullupclub.com 🚌 19

Jazz Club

A club that plays jazz with serious music and appreciative audiences. Obtain membership at the door to enter.

✉ Via Nuova dei Caccini 3 ☎ 055/247 9700; www.jazzclubfirenze.com 🚌 6, 12, 14, 23, 71

Meccanò

This is probably the most popular club in the city, although not the most central; to the west of central Florence, by the Cascine park.

✉ Via dell'Olmo ☎ 055/331 371 🕐 Closed Mon 🚌 17c

Rex

One of the most welcoming of Florence's late-night bar-clubs.

✉ Via Fiesolana 25r ☎ 055/248 0331 🚌 B

Space Electronic

This packed club pulls in the crowds with its eminently danceable range of mainstream rock and pop.

✉ Via Palazzuolo 37 ☎ 055/293 082; www.spaceelectronic.net 🚌 B and D run along part of Via Palazzuolo, a few blocks away from Space Electronic

Tenax

The city's largest dance club, popular with visitors and Florentines alike. It's out in the direction of the airport.

✉ Via Pratese 46a, Peretola ☎ 055/632 958; www.tenax.org 🚌 Best to take a taxi

Yab

Florence's larger clubs and discos tend to be on the city's fringes. Yab attracts both visitors and a local crowd, which, with the familiar dance music, makes for an enjoyable evening.

✉ Via dei Sassetti 5r ☎ 055/215 160; www.yab.it 🚌 In the pedestrian zone

THEATRE

Most Florentine theatrical productions will require a good grasp of Italian. If you want to see one, the city's leading theatres are the Teatro della Pergola (Via della Pergola 18, tel 055/226 4353; www.teatrodellapergola.com), with mainstream classical plays performed by leading Italian companies, and the similar Teatro Verdi (Via Ghibellina 99, tel 055/212 320).

Northern Tuscany

Northern Tuscany is a region of secret corners and little-known towns, a rich and fascinating area often ignored by visitors anxious to explore the more celebrated sights south of Florence.

In Lucca, it has one of the loveliest towns in Italy, a beautiful medley of quiet streets, Romanesque churches, quaint squares and imposing city walls. Nearby Pisa is less charming, but the sights of the Campo dei Miracoli – the famous Leaning Tower, Duomo and Baptistery – make up one of Europe's finest architectural ensembles.

Smaller towns such as Pistoia and Carrara also have their artistic treasures, while Viareggio is a busy but appealing resort if you want a day by the sea. Carrara is also known for its marble, quarried for centuries from the Alpi Apuane. These spectacular mountains form part of the Garfagnana, a varied region of dulcet valleys, wild uplands, lonely lakes and beguiling rural villages.

Pisa

ALPI APUANE

The Apuan Alps contain Tuscany's most spectacular scenery, forming a jagged crest of mountains above the Versilian coast north of Pisa and Lucca. Marble mines streak their western flanks, the source for centuries of stone that has served sculptors from Michelangelo to Henry Moore. On their eastern borders, chestnut-covered slopes fall away to the Garfagnana, a dulcet valley by the pleasant little towns of Barga and Castelnuovo (Barga, in particular, is well worth visiting for its lovely cathedral). Well-marked trails criss-cross the slopes, wending through woods or cresting the panoramic and craggy summit ridges. Excellent walking maps of the region are widely available, making it easy to undertake light strolls or proper hikes. Stazzema and Levigliani make good departure points in the west; late May is the best time to see the area's renowned spring flowers. Driving is also a delight, the excellent folk museum in San Pellegrino in Alpe (16km/10 miles northeast of Castelnuovo) being a particularly good target. The mountains have protected park status, and are earmarked for future national park designation.

✚ 4C 🚉 Pisa to Pietrasanta or Massa; Lucca to Castelnuovo di Garfagnana
🛈 Piazzale Giuseppe Verdi ☎ 0583/442 944 or 0583/583 150

BARGA

Barga is the most interesting village in the Garfagnana, perched high on the slopes of the Orecchiella mountains and looking across the valley to the jagged peaks of the Alpi Apuane. A lovely setting aside, its main attraction is the honey-stoned Duomo, San

Cristofano, founded in the ninth century at the village's highest point, its terrace offering a glorious view over the rooftops to the mountains beyond. Behind a lovely Romanesque façade, the interior contains a sublime pulpit, probably the work of a 13th-century sculptor from Como in northern Italy. Also noteworthy is a large 10th- or 12th-century wooden sculpture of St Christopher. Elsewhere, be sure to visit Santissimo Crocifisso dei Bianchi (irregular hours), an extravagantly decorated baroque chapel just below the Duomo, and the **Museo Civico del Territorio di Barga,** a modest but interesting museum devoted to the region's geological and archaeological history.

➕ 5C 🚉 From Lucca to Barga station, 3.5km (2 miles) from the village
ℹ️ Via di Mezzo 47 ☎ 0583 724 743; www.barganews.com

Museo Civico del Territorio di Barga

✉️ Palazzo Pretorio, Arringo del Duomo ☎ 0583/711 100 🕐 Daily 10–12:30, 2:30–5, but hours may vary ✋ Moderate

CARRARA

The mountains around Carrara have been quarried for their grey-white marble for centuries, and today, with over 200 mines and around 700,000 tonnes of stone extracted a year, the region is the world's largest marble producer. While the mines may blight the surroundings, the centre of hilltop Carrara itself is delightful, full of medieval streets and pretty, pastel-painted stucco houses. Start exploring in Piazza Alberica, the main square, framed by the surrounding hills and close to the town's 11th-century Duomo, whose attractive Pisan-Romanesque façade makes the most of its cramped setting. The interior's artistic highlight is a fine 15th-century pulpit.

Then, either drive or a take a local bus towards Marina di Carrara, to visit the **Museo Civico di Marmo,** an impressive museum that delves into the history and production of the marble. You should also try to venture into the hills immediately around the town to visit some of the working marble mines. The most accessible are signposted off the road to Colonnata, 8km (5 miles) from the town: look for signs saying *Visita Cave* or *Cava di Marmo.* Larger mines can be visited farther south around Monte Corchia.

✚ 3C

Museo Civico di Marmo

✉ Via XX Settembre, 2km (1.2 miles) southwest of town centre 🕒 May–Sep Mon–Sat 9:30–1, 3:30–6; Oct–Apr Mon–Sat 9–12:30, 2:30–5 ✋ Moderate

EMPOLI

Empoli is a predominantly modern, industrial town and rail junction, a place unseen by most visitors, the majority of whom pass through on the train en route for Florence, Pisa or Siena. If you do have an hour to spare, make first for the central Piazza Farinata degli Uberti, named after the leader of the Sienese army that defeated the Florentines at the Battle of Montaperti in 1260. The square's principal historic building is the Collegiata, founded as early as the fifth century, with a venerable, Romanesque lower portion and an upper section that was restored after damage in the Second World War.

Next to the Collegiata is the **Museo della Collegiata,** home to an impressive collection of paintings and sculptures, including triptychs by Lorenzo di Monaco, a rare Pietà by Masolino and sculptures by Tuscan masters Mino da Fiesole and Bernardo Rossellino. There is also a solemn *Annunciation* by Francesco Botticini (1446–1498), who decorated parts of the Collegiata.

Empoli was the birthplace of the composer and pianist Ferruccio Busoni (1866–1924) and commemorates its most famous son with a series of recitals from October to May.

www.comune.empoli.fi.it

➕ 8F

Museo della Collegiata

✉ Piazzetta della Propositora ☎ 0571/76 284 ⏰ Tue–Sun 9–12, 4–7
✋ Inexpensive

GARFAGNANA

The Garfagnana is one of Tuscany's least-visited scenic enclaves, a wonderfully varied region north of Lucca that consists of verdant valleys, pastoral meadows, thick forests, the spectacular peaks of the Alpi Apuane to the west and the more dulcet uplands of the Orecchiella to the east. The region centres on the valley of the Serchio, which carries the area's main road and rail link, as well as the rather lacklustre main town, Castelnuovo di Garfagnana.

You'll need a car, especially if you want to visit the best of the upland villages (notably Barga) or explore the many dramatic and scenic small roads that wind into the

mountains. One of the best roads runs through the hamlet of San Pellegrino in Alpe, 16km (10 miles) east of Castelnuovo, where there is a superb museum of rural life, the **Museo Etnografico Provinciale.**

The same roads can also be used to reach high-level trailheads for some excellent hiking. Both the Alpi Apuane and Orecchiella are protected areas, and have numerous marked trails. Walking maps are available locally. Tuscany's most spectacular cave system, the **Grotta del Vento,** is in Fornovo, 9km (5.5 miles) west of Barga's railway station. However, it can be busy and is rather commercialized.

✚ 5C

ℹ️ Piazza delle Erbe, Castelnuovo di Garfagnana ☎ 0583/65 169

Museo Etnografico Provinciale

✉️ Via del Voltone 14 ☎ 0583/649 072 👋 Inexpensive 🕐 Jul, Aug daily 9:30–1, 2:30–7; Jun, Sep Tue–Sun 9:30–1, 2:30–7; Apr, May Tue–Sun 9–12, 2–5; Oct–Mar Tue–Sat 9–12, Sun 2–5

Grotta del Vento

✉️ Fornovo Lasso ☎ 0583/722 024 🕐 Apr–Oct 1-, 2-, 3-hour tours on the hour 10–6; Nov–Mar 1-hour tours Mon–Sat 10–5

LUCCA

Lucca is one of Tuscany's gems, filled with cobbled streets, tiny Romanesque churches, bristling towers and lovely medieval buildings. The town began life as a Roman colony, later becoming Tuscany's first Christian town and the seat of the region's Imperial rulers (the Margraves). Its medieval wealth was second only to Florence, thanks to its banking and textiles, allowing it to dominate western Tuscany for centuries. Independent until 1799, it passed to Napoleon in 1809 (the town was ruled by his sister, Elisa Baciocchi) and then to the Grand Duchy of Tuscany in 1847.

Walking Lucca's streets is a pleasure in itself, but no trip to the city would be complete without wandering part of the city walls, 4km (2.5 miles) in all, built in the 16th and 17th centuries as a defence against the Tuscan dukes. From their tree-lined ramparts you can enjoy panoramas over the pantiled rooftops, occasionally descending to explore sights such as the peaceful little **L'Orto Botanico** (Botanic Gardens), in the city's southeast corner.

✚ 5E

🛈 Piazzale Giuseppe Verdi ☎ 0583/442 944; www.comune.lucca.it ⏱ Daily 9–7 (5:30pm Nov–Mar)

L'Orto Botanico

✉ Via dell'Orto Botanico 14 ☎ 0583/583 086 ⏱ Jul to mid-Sep Mon–Sat 10–7; May, Jun 10–6; Apr, mid-Sep to mid-Oct 10–5; mid-Oct to Mar by appointment only, Mon–Fri 9:30–12:30 ✋ Inexpensive

Duomo di San Martino

Lucca's stunning Romanesque cathedral is one of Tuscany's architectural masterpieces. The asymmetrical façade, begun in 1070, is famous for its carved reliefs, especially those over the central door – the *Life of St Martin* and *Labours of the Months* – and those of the left portal (1233), probably by Nicola Pisano. Matteo Civitali (1436–1502), a local sculptor, took charge inside, where he was responsible for the inlaid floor, pulpit, water stoups, two tombs in the south transept and the vast *Tempietto* (midway down the nave), an octagonal structure built to house the *Volto Santo*, a 'true effigy' of Christ carved after the Crucifixion (probably a 13th-century fake). This statue, which is robed rather than naked, in the Byzantine style, is carried through the streets of Lucca on the eve of the Feast of the Holy Cross (13 September). The interior's highlight is Jacopo della Quercia's *Tomb of Illaria del Carretto* (1408), one of Italy's most beautiful tombs (it is currently housed off the right nave: there is a small admission charge to view it). The cathedral also contains paintings by Fra Bartolomeo, Bronzino, Tintoretto and Domenico Ghirlandaio. The nearby **Museo della Cattedrale** has a collection of religious and other objects.

Duomo

✉ Piazza San Martino ⏱ Apr–Oct daily 7–7; Nov–Mar 7–5

Museo della Cattedrale

✉ Piazza Antelminelli ☎ 0583/490 530; www.museocattedralelucca.it ⏱ Mid-Mar to Oct daily 10–6; Nov to mid-Mar Mon–Fri 10–2, Sat, Sun 10–5 ✋ Moderate. Joint ticket with Church of San Giovanni

Museo Nazionale di Villa Guinigi

The Museo Nazionale di Villa Guinigi, at the eastern end of the town, has a major collection of sculpture, paintings and archaeological fragments, including objects dating back to the Etruscan and Roman periods. Among the exhibits are works by Jacopo della Quercia, Matteo Civitali, Fra Bartolomeo and paintings by anonymous Sienese and Lucchese masters. More paintings can be seen across the city in the **Pinacoteca Nazionale,** housed in the Palazzo Mansi, a wonderful rococo palace.

✉ Via della Quarquonia ☎ 0583/496 033 ◷ Tue–Sat 8:30–7:30, Sun 8:30–1:30 ✋ Moderate, or expensive for joint ticket with Pinacoteca Nazionale di Palazzo Mansi

Pinacoteca Nazionale di Palazzo Mansi

✉ Via Galli Tassi 43 ☎ 0583/55 570 or 0583/583 461 ◷ Tue–Sat 8:30–7, Sun and public hols 8:30–1 ✋ Moderate, or expensive for joint ticket with Villa Guinigi

San Frediano

San Frediano (1112–47), the third of Lucca's major churches, is dominated by a superb 13th-century façade mosaic, while the dark interior features a wealth of sculptures and paintings. One of the main attractions is the magnificent *Fonta Lustrale*, a large and intricately carved 12th-century font. Behind it, a carved *Annunciation* by Andrea della Robbia is framed by festoons of terracotta fruit. Close by is the tomb of St Zita, patron saint of serving maids. The Cappella Trenta (fourth chapel on the left) features two floor tombs and a sculpted altarpiece (1422) by Jacopo della Quercia; the second chapel in the same aisle contains the city's best fresco cycle – Amico Aspertini's 16th-century scenes from the lives of San Frediano and St Augustine – as well as the *Arrival of the Volto Santo in Lucca.*

Just to the southeast of the church is Piazza Anfiteatro, an evocative square whose oval of crumbling houses mirrors the shape of the Roman amphitheatre that stood here until the 12th

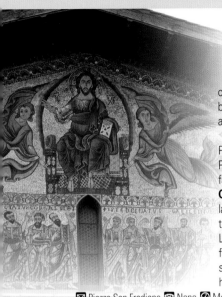

century. Many were partly built with stone from the amphitheatre.

A short distance south of Piazza Anfiteatro (walk via San Pietro Somaldi for its lovely façade) brings you to the **Torre Guinigi,** an eccentric city landmark built as a defensive tower by the Guinigi, one of Lucca's leading medieval families. A grove of ilex trees sprouts from its summit, and it has lovely views over the city.

✉ Piazza San Frediano ☎ None 🕐 Mon–Sat 8:30–12, 3–5, Sun 10:30–5 (except during services) ✋ Free

Torre Guinigi

✉ Via Sant'Andrea 41 ☎ 0583/316 846 🕐 Jul to mid-Sep daily 9am–midnight; Apr, May, mid-Sep to Oct 9–9; Mar 9–7; Nov–Feb 9:30–6 ✋ Moderate

San Michele in Foro

Lucca's streets focus on Piazza San Michele, site of the old Roman forum (foro), and now home to San Michele, one of Italy's loveliest churches. Some 300 years in the making, its façade is a wonderful confection of pillars, arcades and tiny twisted columns. The interior, by contrast, is plain, apart from a della Robbia terracotta and Filippino Lippi's *Saints Jerome, Sebastian, Roch and Helena*. West of the square lies the **Casa Natale di Puccini,** birthplace of Giacomo Puccini (1858–1924), currently closed. There is a monument to Lucca's war dead just off Piazza Napoleone.

✉ Piazza San Michele ☎ None 🕐 Daily 7:40–12, 3–6. Closed 1 Jan, 25 Dec ✋ Free

MONTECATINI TERME

Montecatini Terme is one of Italy's most popular and exclusive spa towns. The nine natural sulphur springs, each with its own building, are in the Parco delle Terme, dominated by the Terme Leopoldine. The town's belle époque architecture adds to the refined atmosphere. Even if you are not taking a full cure in one of the town's many hotels, you can sample the waters in the spa café. There is little to see in the town, but it is fun to ride the funicular (Apr–Oct only) to Montecatini Alto, the town's original medieval heart, where Piazza Giusti offers some fine views.

www.montecatiniturismo.it

✚ 7E 🛈 Viale Verdi 66 ☎ 0572/772 244

PISA

Pisa has more to offer than its famous leaning tower (➤ 54–55), not least the ensemble of sights on Piazza dei Miracoli, the broad grassy square that encloses not only the tower but also the town's cathedral, Baptistery and Camposanto. Begun in 1153, the **Baptistery** (Italy's largest) is a mixture of Romanesque and Gothic, the latter added by Nicola and Giovanni Pisano between 1270 and

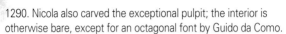

1290. Nicola also carved the exceptional pulpit; the interior is otherwise bare, except for an octagonal font by Guido da Como.

The **cathedral** is earlier, dating from 1063, though most of the interior was remodelled after a disastrous fire in 1595. Among the survivors of the conflagration were the bronze doors (1180) and Giovanni Pisano's majestic pulpit. The piazza's third component, the marble-walled **Camposanto,** is a medieval cemetery whose once famous frescoes were all but obliterated by Allied bombing in 1944. Its tombs and fragments, however, are still worth a visit.

Bombing destroyed much else in Pisa, but spared the exhibits of the **Museo dell'Opera del Duomo,** a 23-room museum with an uneven collection of paintings, sculptures and other objects. The **Museo Nazionale di San Matteo,** Pisa's main civic museum, is similarly hit-and-miss, but includes works by Masaccio, Donatello and Simone Martini. The town's loveliest church is Santa Maria della Spina, named after a spine *(spina)* from Christ's Crown of Thorns kept inside.

www.pisaturismo.it

✚ 13G

ℹ Piazza Arcivescadovo ☎ 050/42 291

Duomo, Baptistery, Camposanto and Museo dell'Opera

✉ Campo (Piazza) dei Miracoli ☎ 050/560 547 (all sights); www.opapisa.it

🕐 Duomo: late Mar to end Sep daily 10–8; Oct 10–7; Nov–Feb 10–1, 2–5; early Mar 9–6; mid-Mar 10–7.

Baptistery, Camposanto, Museo dell'Opera: late Mar to Sep daily 8–8; Oct 9–7; Nov–Feb 10–5; early Mar 9–6; mid-Mar 9–7

💷 Inexpensive (single ticket); also a variety of combined tickets

Museo Nazionale di San Matteo

✉ Lungarno Mediceo ☎ 050/541 865 🕐 Mon–Sat 9–7, Sun 9–2

💷 Expensive

PISTOIA

Pistoia's industrial outskirts deter most visitors, which is a shame, for the town boasts a medieval centre and a group of churches and monuments that stand comparison with any in Tuscany. Piazza del Duomo, its captivating main square, is home to the Campanile, a former Lombard watchtower; several medieval palaces; a 14th-century baptistery; and the arched façade of the town's **cathedral.**

The last contains a font by Benedetto da Maiano (entrance wall) and the tomb of Cino da Pistoia (1337), writer and friend of Dante. The chief highlight is the St James Altar (1287–1456), Italy's finest piece of medieval silverware. The work contains some 628 figures and depicts episodes from the Old and New Testaments. To the left and rear of the cathedral is the **Museo Civico,** with a collection of paintings and sculptures.

Elsewhere in the town be sure to see the 12th-century church of San Bartolomeo in Pantano, which has a pulpit (1250) by Guido da Como; San Giovanni Fuorcivitas, known for its pulpit by Guglielmo da Pisa (1270); and Sant'Andrea, also famous for its pulpit (1301), an outstanding work by Giovanni Pisano. Sculpture of a different kind adorns the façade of the Ospedale del Ceppo, a 13th-century hospital decorated with a colourful glazed terracotta frieze (1514–25) by Giovanni della Robbia (The Seven Works of Mercy). Finally, visit the Cappella del Tau, a deconsecrated church noted for its 14th-century Gothic frescoes.

www.comune.pistoia.it

➕ 8D

ℹ️ Palazzo dei Vescovi, Piazza del Duomo 4 ☎ 0573/21 622

Cathedral

✉️ Piazza del Duomo ☎ 0573/25 095 🕐 Daily 8–12:30, 4–7 ✋ Cathedral: free. St James Altar: inexpensive

Museo Civico

✉️ Palazzo del Comune, Piazza del Duomo ☎ 0573/371 296 🕐 Apr–Oct Tue, Thu–Sat 10–6, Wed 4–7, Sun 11–6; Nov–Mar Tue, Thu–Sat 10–5, Wed 3–6, Sun 11–5. Closed Mon ✋ Inexpensive

PRATO

Prato is Tuscany's largest city after Florence, its wealth founded on a centuries-old textile industry, which continues today. It receives few visitors, yet its modern suburbs enclose a perfectly preserved historic heart, bounded by old walls and filled with architectural and artistic treasures. The main sights are the **Castello dell'Imperatore,** begun around 1230 for Emperor Frederick II, the Renaissance church of Santa Maria delle Carceri, and the Duomo, known for its **museum,** Filippo Lippi's frescoes (1452–66) around the high altar, a fresco cycle (1392–5) by Agnolo Gaddi and a magnificent pulpit by Michelozzo and Donatello.

www.pratoturismo.it

➕ 9E

ℹ️ Piazza del Duomo 8 🕐 0574/24 112

Museo dell'Opera del Duomo

✉️ Piazza del Duomo 49 ☎ 0574/29 339 🕐 Mon, Wed–Sat 10–1, 3–6:30, Sun 10–1. Closed Tue ✋ Moderate. Combined ticket with Castello available

Castello dell'Imperatore

✉️ Viale Piave ☎ 0574/38 207 🕐 Apr–Sep Mon, Wed–Sat 9–1, 4–7; Oct–Mar Mon, Wed–Sun 9–1. Closed Tue ✋ Inexpensive

VIAREGGIO

Tuscany's main seaside resort is just an hour or so by train from Florence, and in summer it is often full of Florentines escaping the city's bustle. This can make it busy, but rarely unpleasant, for the resort has a distinctly elegant air, thanks to long avenues of palms, numerous large stucco-fronted hotels, an airy waterfront promenade, and a handful of Liberty-style frontages. Most of the last are at the eastern end of Viale Regina Margherita, the town's long waterfront boulevard, clustered around the Gran Caffè Margherita, a historic café. The beaches are well groomed, but note that most are private concessions *(stabilimenti)*, where an entry fee of a few euros buys you the rental of towels and a sun-lounger plus bar, restaurant and bathroom facilities.

www.aptversilia.it

✚ 4E

ℹ️ Viale Carducci 10 ☎ 0584/962 233. There is also a seasonal information kiosk (Apr–Sep) at the railway station ☎ 0584/46 382

HOTELS

LUCCA

Locanda S Agostino (€€)

This beautifully renovated medieval mansion is a low-key and relaxing place to stay. Rooms are individually decorated and have LCD TV, DVD player and Wi-Fi. There's a walled garden where you can relax over an espresso or two.

✉ Piazza S Agostino 3 ☎ 0538/467 884; www.locandasantagostino.it

La Luna (€)

La Luna is centrally located close to the evocative Piazza Anfiteatro. The rooms are a mixture of old and new, some with wooden ceilings.

✉ Corte Compagni 12, off Via Fillungo ☎ 0583/493 634; www.hotellaluna.com

Piccolo Hotel Puccini (€)

A splendid central position close to Piazza San Michele. Pleasant and well-presented rooms, though the communal parts are a little cramped. The house in which Puccini was born, now a museum, is just opposite.

✉ Via di Poggio 9 ☎ 0583/55 421; www.hotelpuccini.com

PISA

Touring (€)

This is one of the best of a crop of impersonal hotels around the station. The rooms are not terribly large, but all are modern and functional.

✉ Via Puccini 24 (off the northeast flank of Piazza della Stazione)
☎ 050/46 374; www.hoteltouringpisa.com

PISTOIA

Leon Bianco (€–€€)

In a central and reasonably peaceful position just south of Piazza del Duomo. Rooms on Via Cavour are perhaps less appealing than those away from the street.

✉ Via Panciatichi 2 ☎ 0573/26 675; www.hotelleonbianco.it

RESTAURANTS

BARGA
L'Altana (€)
A good, basic trattoria always full of locals eating traditional food made with locally sourced ingredients and backed up with local wines. The menu is seasonal and service is friendly.
✉ Via di Mezzo 1 ☎ 0583/723 194 or 713 192 🕓 Tue–Sun

COLONNATA
Venanzio (€€)
An intimate and elegant restaurant that offers sophisticated regional dishes. Located in the village of Colonnata, 7km (4 miles) from Carrara, at the heart of the marble-mining region.
✉ Piazza Palestro 3, Colonnata ☎ 0585/758 033 🕓 Closed Sun evening, except Aug

EMPOLI
Il Galeone (€€)
As the name suggests, 'The Galleon' serves a wide range of seafood, with various pastas. There are fresh oysters in season.
✉ Via Curtatone e Montanara 67 ☎ 0571/72 826; www.ristoranteilgaleone.com 🕓 Mon–Sat 12–3, 7:30–10:30. Closed Sun

LUCCA
La Buca di Sant'Antonio (€€)
Once the city's coaching house, this restaurant offers traditional cooking, a central location and a pleasant atmosphere. It's a winning combination. Dishes include *bacalà*, delicate *ravioli di ricotta* and *risotto*.
✉ Via della Cervia 1–3 ☎ 0583/55 881; www.bucadisantantonio.com
🕓 Closed Sun evening, Mon and parts of Jan and Jul

Da Leo Fratelli Buralli (€)
A busy, no-frills trattoria that provides Lucchese workers with a reasonably priced lunch. The cooking has Tuscan-Lucchese leanings.
✉ Via Tegrimi 1 ☎ 0583/492 236; www.trattoriadaleo.it 🕓 Closed Sun evening

Osteria Baralla (€–€€)

A few steps from the Piazza dell'Anfiteatro, this simple, popular restaurant serves unpretentious regional dishes at fair prices.

✉ Via dell'Anfiteatro 5 ☎ 0583/440 240; www.osteriabaralla.it

🕐 Closed Sun

PISA

Antica Trattoria da Bruno (€€)

This bustling and friendly restaurant is a family affair, where you'll find a good range of Tuscan dishes. Autumn specialties include game dishes and excellent *funghi* (mushrooms), while good fresh fish is available year-round. Reservations are advisable.

✉ Via Bianchi 12 ☎ 050/560 818; www.anticatrattoriadabruno.com

🕐 Closed Tue

Il Campano (€€)

A fine restaurant with homemade pastas and excellent fish and seafood dishes, between the River Arno and Piazza dei Cavalieri.

✉ Via Domenico Cavalca 44 ☎ 050/580 585 🕐 Closed Wed

Osteria dei Cavalieri (€–€€)

This has traditionally been one of the best-known and better regarded of Pisa's handful of central restaurants. Cooking is not especially distinguished, but the food is mostly reliable, fresh and well prepared. The choice of wines is good, and service generally jovial and accomplished. It's on the street running south from Piazza dei Cavalieri. Reservations may be needed in high season.

✉ Via San Frediano 16 ☎ 050/580 858; www.osteriacavalieri.pisa.it

🕐 Closed Sat lunch and Sun; also Aug, 30 Dec–7 Jan

PISTOIA

San Jacopo (€€)

A thoroughly reliable choice in the historic part of town for venerable Tuscan dishes, including some unique to Pistoia, such as *maccheroni sull'anatra muta* (pasta with duck sauce), traditionally eaten on the feast day of the city's patron saint.

✉ Via Crispi 15 ☎ 0573/27 786 🕐 Closed Tue lunch and Mon

PRATO
Osteria Cibbè (€)

A small and pleasantly rustic *osteria* in a medieval town house, with marble tables, terracotta floors and vaulted ceilings. Offers simple, classic Tuscan cuisine. Outdoor dining possible in summer.

✉ Piazza Mercatale 49 ☎ 0574/607 509 🕓 Closed Sun and some of Aug

SHOPPING

ARTS AND CRAFTS

Most Tuscan towns have at least one shop selling ceramics and terracotta. Lucca, Pisa and the towns of the Versilia Coast (Massa and Carrara) have many outlets selling the marble for which the region is famous. Linens and textiles are another good buy, with Lucca, in particular, having been renowned for centuries for its silk.

MARKETS
Lucca

The market in Via dei Bacchettoni, on the town's eastern fringes, sells clothing, food and household goods. Arrive early for the best bargains. The Piazza del Carmine market is a covered food market.

✉ Via dei Bacchettoni 🕓 Daily
✉ Piazza del Carmine 🕓 Wed and Sat am

Pistoia

A regular fruit and veg market, frequented by local residents.

✉ Piazza della Sala 🕓 Daily

ENTERTAINMENT

CLASSICAL MUSIC
Festival Pucciniano

The Festival Pucciniano is a series of outdoor concerts featuring the music of Puccini, held in July and August at Torre del Lago (near Lucca), where he once lived. Lucca itself stages the major Sagra Musicale Lucchese, a wide-ranging summer arts festival, from April to July.

✉ Fondazione Festival Pucciniano, Torre del Lago ☎ Information: 0584/350 567. Box office: 0584/359 322; www.puccinifestival.it 🕓 Aug

Southern Tuscany

Mention Tuscany, and Southern Tuscany is the region that readily comes to mind, filled with the classic landscapes of olive groves, vineyards, cypress-topped hills and poppy-filled fields, and scattered with elegant villas, pretty farmhouses and countless sun-hazed hill towns.

Siena

At its heart is Siena, the finest medieval town in Europe, centred on the Campo, its majestic square, best known as the stage for the twice-yearly Palio horse race. Elsewhere, virtually every town has something of interest – Arezzo, Cortona, Montalcino, Pienza, San Gimignano, Volterra – as do the region's many pockets of glorious countryside, notably the wooded hills of Chianti and the pastoral heartlands south of Siena, each graced with pretty villages, sweeping views and beautiful, ancient abbeys such as Sant'Antimo and Monte Oliveto Maggiore.

ABBAZIA DI MONTE OLIVETO MAGGIORE

Tuscany's finest working monastery was founded in the 14th century by the Olivetans, an offshoot of the Benedictines, and is set in glorious countryside, with sweeping views. Much of the large abbey complex remains closed to visitors, but you are able to see the Chiostro Grande, or Grand Cloister, among other things, which is home to a majestic fresco cycle on the *Life of St Benedict*, painted between 1497 and 1505 by Luca Signorelli and Antonio Bazzi, better known as Il Sodoma. The cycle's many panels contain a wealth of wonderful narrative detail. Be sure to see the finely carved choir stalls (1500–20) in the baroque abbey church.
www.monteolivetomaggiore.it

✚ 20L

✉ Monte Oliveto Maggiore, Chiusure, near Buonconvento ☎ 0577/707 652
🕐 Daily 9:15–12, 3:15–6 (5 in winter) ✋ Free

AREZZO

This largely modern town merits a visit for Piero della Francesca's *The Legend of the True Cross* (1452–66), one of the most famous fresco cycles in Italy. Ranged across the chancel of the church of **San Francesco,** in the old town, the cycle describes how the tree from which Eve plucked the forbidden fruit becomes Christ's cross. Although damaged in places, the frescoes have been restored, emphasizing the calm tones and subtlety for which Piero is known.

The Piazza Grande, the town's precipitously sloping main square, is graced by the Loggia di Vasari (1573) and Palazzetto della Fraternità della Laici, built for a lay confraternity and distinguished by a beautiful doorway and lunette tabernacle (1434) by Bernardino Rossellino. To its left protrudes the arcaded apse of Santa Maria, a Romanesque church whose façade overlooks the Corso Italia. The interior has a superb altarpiece (1320) by Pietro Lorenzetti.

To the north stands the **Duomo,** whose airy Gothic interior is known for Piero della Francesca's fresco of *Mary Magdalene* and 14th-century *Tomb of Bishop Guido Tarlati* (end of the north aisle). Also worth a look are the cathedral museum, filled with paintings, sculpture and terracotta; the nearby **Casa Vasari,** birthplace of the 16th-century painter and writer; and the **Museo d'Arte Medievale e Moderna,** with an eclectic assortment of paintings and objects, including five rooms of ceramics and paintings by the *Macchiaioli,* the so-called 'Italian Impressionists'.

www.apt.arezzo.it

✚ 22J

🛈 Piazza della Repubblica 28 ☎ 0575/377 678

San Francesco

✉ Piazza San Francesco ☎ 0575/299 071 or 0575/352 727 🕔 Apr–Oct Mon–Fri 9–6:30, Sat 9–5:30, Sun 1–5:30; Nov–Mar Mon–Fri 9–5:30, Sat 9–5, Sun 1–5. Prebooked guided tours every 30 mins 🖐 Moderate. Tickets must be prebooked by phone, online at www.apt.arezzo.it or (off-season) in person at least an hour before visit

Duomo

✉ Piazza del Duomo ☎ 0575/23 991 🕔 Daily 6:30–12:30, 3–6:30 🖐 Free

Casa Vasari

✉ Via XX Settembre 55 ☎ 0575/409 040 🕔 Apr–Oct Wed–Mon 8:30–7:30; Nov–Mar Wed–Mon 8:30–1. Closed Tue 🖐 Inexpensive

Museo d'Arte Medievale e Moderna

✉ Via di San Lorentino 8 ☎ 0575/409 050 🕔 Tue–Sun 8:30–7. Closed Mon and 1 Jan, 1 May, 25 Dec 🖐 Moderate

CORTONA

Etruscan Cortona is a beguiling little hill town, with ancient walls ringed with olives and vineyards. A short walk from Piazza della Repubblica, which forms the heart of the old town, leads to

the **Museo Diocesano,** noted for a handful of Renaissance paintings. The best-known are the glorious *Annunciation* (1428–30) and *Madonna Enthroned with Saints*, both by Fra Angelico.

The town's other major gallery is the **Museo dell'Accademia Etrusca e della Città Cortona,** packed with a wide-ranging collection of Etruscan objects, Renaissance ivories, porcelain, ceramics, miniatures, coins and jewellery. Its highlights are an unusual 5th-century BC Etruscan 'chandelier' and a reconstructed Etruscan tomb.

You should also visit San Niccolò, approached through a little walled garden and dominated by an intriguing double-sided altarpiece by Luca Signorelli. San Domenico has another work by Signorelli, a *Madonna and Saints*, while San Francesco boasts a fine *Annunciation* by Pietro da Cortona. Some way outside the walls stands Santa Maria del Calcinaio, a distinguished but rather austere Renaissance church. A far better destination if you want to stretch your legs is the Fortezza Medicea, a ruined Medici fortress at the top of the town, which offers sensational views across Lake Trasimeno and the Umbrian hills.

www.comunedicortona.it

🔁 22K

ℹ️ Palazzo Casali, Piazza Signorelli ☎ 0575/637 221

Museo Diocesano

✉️ Piazza del Duomo 1 ☎ 0575/62 830 🕐 Apr–Sep daily 10–7; Oct Tue–Sun 10–7; Nov–Mar Tue–Sun 10–5 💰 Moderate

Museo dell'Accademia Etrusca e della Città Cortona
✉ Palazzo Casali, Piazza Signorelli 19 ☎ 0575/637 235; www.cortonamaec.org
🕐 Apr–Oct daily 10–7; Nov–Mar Tue–Sun 10–5 ✋ Expensive

MONTALCINO

Lofty Montalcino is one of Tuscany's most pleasing hill towns, with picture-perfect streets, magnificent views and some of the best wine in Italy. A fairy-tale **fortezza** (fortress) dominates the town's southern approaches, begun in 1361 and strengthened by Cosimo I in 1571 after the town had fallen to the Medici (Montalcino was the last town of the Sienese Republic to surrender to Florence). Inside is a little wine bar where you can sample local wines, along with a watchtower and battlements with far-reaching views.

You can also buy wines at the Fiaschetteria Italiana, a pretty, turn-of-the century café in Piazza del Popolo, the town's modest main square. On one side of the square stands the narrow Palazzo dei Priori (1292), on another the graceful arches of a Renaissance loggia. The town's new **Museo Civico** is housed in a monastery annexed to the fresco-filled church of Sant'Agostino. The museum

is full of valuable wooden sculptures and wonderful Gothic and Renaissance paintings.

A few kilometres south of Montalcino lies **Sant'Antimo,** a superb Cistercian abbey in glorious pastoral countryside and reputedly founded by Charlemagne in the late 700s, though most of the present Romanesque building dates from the 12th century. The stunning interior features several finely carved capitals: look for the second column on the right, where the capital shows *Daniel in the Lion's Den.*

✚ 20M

ℹ Costa del Municipio 1 ☎ 0577/849 331; www.prolocomontalcino.it

Fortezza

✉ Piazzale della Fortezza ☎ 0577/849 211 🕐 Apr–Oct daily 9–8; Nov–Mar
Tue–Sat 9–6 ✋ Moderate; joint ticket with Museo Civico 🍴 Wine and
snacks from the *enoteca* (€)

Museo Civico

✉ Via Ricasoli 31 ☎ 0577/846 014 🕐 Tue–Sun 10–1, 2–5:50
✋ Moderate

Sant'Antimo

✉ 1km (half a mile) from Castelnuovo dell'Abate ☎ 0577/835 659
🕐 Mon–Sat 10–12:30, 3–6:30, Sun 9–10:30, 3–6 ✋ Free

MONTEPULCIANO

Ancient Montepulciano is the highest of the Tuscan hill towns,
gazing down across Lake Trasimeno and Umbria's hazy hills. Strung
along a narrow ridge, the town hinges around a single main street –
the Corso – a precipitous climb which passes a succession of
interesting churches and Renaissance palaces. Look for Palazzo
Cocconi (No 70), attributed to Antonio Sangallo; Vignola's Palazzo
Tarugi (No 82); and the Palazzo Bucelli (No 73), whose lower walls
are studded with ancient Etruscan funerary urns.

Further up the hill you pass Michelozzo's Sant'Agostino, and
short detours take you to Santa Lucia and San Francesco. Pop in to
the **Museo Civico,** home to a selection of Gothic and Renaissance
works, and then recover your breath in the Piazza Grande, the
town's main square. Here, the Palazzo Comunale's **tower** provides
good views, while at Palazzo Cantucci, you can buy the town's
famous red wine, *Vino Nobile di Montepulciano*.

Also here is the Duomo, whose high altar shelters Taddeo di
Bartolo's radiant *Assumption* (1401). The baptistery chapel (first
on the left) features a font and six bas-reliefs (1340) by Giovanni
d'Agostino and a della Robbia terracotta that frames a relief of the
Madonna and Child attributed to Benedetto da Maiano.

Leave time for the short walk southwest, beyond the town walls, to **San Biagio,** a celebrated Renaissance church (1518–45) designed by Antonio Sangallo the Elder.

www.prolocomontepulciano.it; www.comune.montepulciano.si.it

✚ 21L

🛈 Piazzale Don Minzoni ☎ 0578/757 341

Museo Civico

✉ Via Ricci 10 ☎ 0578/717 300 🕓 Apr–Oct Tue–Sun 10–7; Nov–Mar Tue–Sun 10–1, 3–6 ✋ Moderate

Torre Comunale

✉ Palazzo Comunale, Piazza Grande 1 ☎ 0578/757 442 or 757 034 🕓 Call for times ✋ Inexpensive

San Biagio

✉ Via di San Biagio 14 ☎ None 🕓 Daily 9–12, 3–6 ✋ Free

PIENZA

Pienza owes much of its present appearance to Aeneas Piccolomini, later Pope Pius II, who tried to turn his birthplace into a model Renaissance town. The transformation began in 1459, a year after he became pope, and was overseen by Bernardo Rossellino. Pius died before his dream was realized, and only the cathedral, a papal lodging and a handful of palaces were ever built.

Piazza Pio II is the heart of the town, dominated by the façade of the **Duomo.** The lofty interior – now showing alarming signs of collapse – was inspired by German 'hall churches' Pius had seen on his travels around Europe. The tall windows – another papal whim – were designed to create a flood of light, symbolizing the enlightenment of the age. Pius also commissioned the five beautiful Sienese altarpieces ranged around the walls.

To the right is the **Palazzo Piccolomini,** Pius's palace, with its glorious triple-tiered loggia and some breathtaking views from the gardens. Rooms open to the public include the papal bedroom and weapon-filled Sala d'Armi. Down the Corso Il Rossellino, just past the Piazza Pio II, is the **Museo Diocesano di Pienza,** with tapestries, manuscripts, silverware and Sienese paintings.

Don't miss the Pieve di Corsignano, an ancient parish church five minutes' walk from Pienza.

www.comunedipienza.it

✚ 21M

🛈 Corso il Rossellino 30 ☎ 0578/749 071, 0578/749 905

Duomo

✉ Piazza Pio II ☎ 0578/749 071 🕐 Daily 8–1, 3–7 ✋ Free

Palazzo Piccolomini

✉ Piazza Pio II ☎ 0578/286 300; www.piazzapiccolominipienza.it 🕐 Mid-Mar to mid-Oct Tue–Sun 10–6:30; mid-Oct to mid-Mar Tue–Sun 10–4:30. Closed early Jan to mid-Feb and last two weeks in Nov ✋ Inexpensive

Museo Diocesano di Pienza

✉ Corso Il Rossellino 30 ☎ 0578/748 379 🕐 Mid-Mar to Oct Wed–Mon 10–1, 3–7; Nov to mid-Mar Sat, Sun 10–1, 3–6 ✋ Moderate

SAN GIMIGNANO

Tuscany's most famous village is a picture of medieval perfection,
its famous towers rising above orange-tiled houses. Two superb
churches, swathed with frescoes, add to its charm; only the
summer's immense crowds detract from the village's appeal. An
Etruscan and then a Roman settlement, it enjoyed its heyday
during the Middle Ages, when its position, close to trade and
pilgrimage routes, brought great prosperity. Family rivalries and the
Black Death brought its eventual downfall, and in 1348 the village
surrendered itself to the protection of Florence. Thereafter it
became a sleepy backwater until the arrival of tourism last century.

A combined San Gimignano ticket gives admission to the
Museo Civico, Torre Grossa, Cappella di Santa Fina (Collegiata),
Museo Archeologico-Spezieria di Santa Fina and Museo
Ornitologico (a museum of stuffed birds south of the Rocca).

www.sangimignano.com

✚ 17J

🛈 Piazza del Duomo 1 ☎ 0577/940 008

Collegiata

Best places to see, pages 38–39.

Museo d'Arte Sacra

An arch to the left of the Collegiata leads to San Gimignano's Baptistery, whose loggia is frescoed with an *Annunciation* (1482) by Ghirlandaio and Sebastiano Mainardi. The courtyard here contains the entrance to the Museo d'Arte Sacra, a modest museum with Etruscan remains, a *Madonna and Child* by Bartolo de Fredi, an early wooden Crucifix, exquisite illuminated choir books, and a marble bust of Onofrio di Pietro (1493), a local scholar, by Benedetto da Maiano.

✉ Piazza Pecori ☎ 0577/940 316 🕒 Apr–Oct Mon–Fri 9:30–7:10, Sat 9:30–5:10, Sun 12:30–5:10; Mar, Nov to mid-Jan Mon–Sat 9:30–4:40, Sun 12:30–4:40. Closed late Jan–Feb ✋ Inexpensive. Admission also by combined ticket

Museo Civico/Torre Grossa

San Gimignano's principal museum is entered through a lovely courtyard, with a loggia partly covered in frescoes by Sodoma and Taddeo di Bartolo. After climbing the stairs you can either enter the museum or climb the Torre Grossa.

The museum's first room (downstairs) is the frescoed Sala di Dante, so-called because the poet spoke here in 1300 during a diplomatic mission from Florence. Its highlight is Lippo Memmi's *Maestà* (1317). Stairs lead to the picture gallery with a large salon and several smaller rooms on the right and one tiny stone-walled room to the left. Here are three frescoes (1320) showing a husband and wife playing and taking a shared bath before climbing into bed.

In the other rooms are outstanding paintings by Filippino Lippi, Pintoricchio and Benozzo Gozzoli, as well as several polyptychs describing the lives of saints Fina and San Gimignano (two of the village patron saints), and a crucifixion by Coppo di Marcovaldo.

✉ Piazza del Duomo ☎ 0577/990 312 🕒 Tower and museum: Mar–Oct daily 9:30–7; Nov–Feb 10–5:30 ✋ Combined ticket for museum and tower: moderate. Combined ticket for museum, tower, Museo Ornitologico and Galleria d'Arte Moderna e Contemporanea: expensive

Piazza della Cisterna

Most people approach central San Gimignano from Porta San Giovanni in the south. From here Via San Giovanni leads past San Francesco, a deconsecrated Pisan-Romanesque church which now serves as a *cantina* selling the village's celebrated white wine (➤ 15). Be sure to walk to the lovely little garden at the back for superb views. At the end of the street you enter Piazza della Cisterna, one of the village's two linked main squares (the other is Piazza del Duomo). The piazza takes its name from the public cistern (1273) which sits at its heart, though the square is more noteworthy for the various medieval palaces and towers on all sides.

Rocca

A short walk from Piazza del Duomo takes you to the Rocca, San Gimignano's old fortress, built in 1353 on the orders of the Florentines. Two centuries later another Florentine, Cosimo I, ordered its destruction (just one of the original towers survives). Today the ruins enclose a pleasant little park with sweeping views from the old ramparts.

Sant'Agostino

The church of Sant'Agostino, begun in 1298, is best known for Benozzo Gozzoli's chancel frescoes of scenes from the *Life of St Augustine* (1463–7). The striking high altar painting, the *Coronation of the Virgin* (1483), is the work of Piero del Pollaiolo; the frescoes on the *Life of the Virgin* (1356) on the walls of the chapel right of the high altar are by Bartolo di Fredi.

The rear wall contains the Cappella di San Bartolo (on the left as you enter), celebrated for its magnificent altar (1495) by Benedetto da Maiano. Its reliefs depict three miracles by San Bartolo, one of the village patron saints, who is buried in the chapel. The three figures above portray the Theological Virtues; Sebastiano Mainardi's frescoes, to the left, show saints Lucy, Nicholas of Bari and Gimignano, the last holding the village of San Gimignano in his arms. The four half-figures (1318) on the church's left wall, by Mino da Fiesole, are believed to be part of Bartolo's original shrine. On the right (south) wall are several notable frescoes, including a *Madonna and Child with Eight Saints* (1494) by Pier Francesco Fiorentino and *Christ with the Symbols of the Passion* by Bartolo di Fredi.

South of the church in the old Santa Fina convent is the **Museo Archeologico,** with Roman and Etrusan finds and the Spezieria di Santa Fina, a medieval pharmacy.

Sant'Agostino

✉ Piazza Sant'Agostino ☎ None ⏰ Apr–Oct daily 7:30–12, 3–7; Nov–Mar 7:30–12, 3–6 💷 Free

Museo Archeologico

✉ Via Folgore 11 ☎ 0577/941 388 ⏰ Daily 11–5:30
💷 Moderate

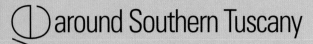

a drive around Southern Tuscany

Leave San Gimignano (► 162–165) and drive on minor roads southeast to Colle di Val d'Elsa (14km/9 miles). Continue to Monteriggioni (9km/6miles) before meeting the Florence–Siena superstrada. Follow this to Siena (► 168–173), then take the city's ring road south before picking up the SP326 (22km/14 miles) for Sinalunga.

Colle di Val d'Elsa is unattractive on its outskirts but retains a beguiling medieval centre with the Duomo, San Francesco and a clutch of smaller churches and museums all worth seeing. Unmissable Monteriggioni is a perfect village, with a couple of streets, old walls and towers.

Follow the SP326 briefly before turning right (south) on the minor 438 to Asciano (20km/12 miles). From Asciano take minor lanes south to Monte Oliveto Maggiore (9km/6 miles), then continue to Buonconvento (9km/6 miles) and south to Montalcino (14km/ 9 miles) and Sant'Antimo (10km/6 miles, ► 157).

The road to Asciano takes you through the *crete*, the Sienese 'badlands', a region of bare clay hills and distant views. Stop at the abbey of Monte Oliveto, famous for its fresco cycles by Sodoma and Luca Signorelli.

From Sant'Antimo take minor roads east towards the main SR2 (21km/13 miles) past the village of Castiglione d'Orcia. Turn left on the SR2 and detour briefly to Bagno Vignoni (2km/1 mile), known for the old spa pool in its main square. Then visit the famous Romanesque Collegiata at San Quirico d'Orcia (6km/4 miles) before picking up the SP146 east to Pienza (10km/6 miles, ► 160) and Montepulciano (13km/8 miles, ► 158–159).

Distance 160km (99 miles)
Time 1–2 days depending on stops
Start point San Gimignano 🕂 17J
End point Montepulciano 🕂 21L
Lunch Taverna Grappolo Blu (€–€€) ✉ Via Scala di Moglio 1, off
Via Mazzini, Montalcino ☎ 0577/847 150
🛈 Colle di Val d'Elsa, Piazza Arnolfo di Cambio 9 ☎ 0577/921 334
(closed Feb and am Nov–Mar)
Asciano Corso Matteotti 18 ☎ 0577/719 510 (summer only)
San Quirico d'Orcia Via Dante Alighieri 33 ☎ 0577/897 211
(summer only)

SIENA

Siena is Italy's loveliest medieval city. Originally
Etruscan, it became a Roman colony and later the
capital of a medieval republic and the principal rival
to Florence. Italy's finest piazza, the Campo, forms
its heart, providing the stage for the Palio, a
famous annual horse race. Here, too, is the Palazzo
Pubblico, home to some of the city's greatest
works of art. Nearby lie the Duomo, one of Italy's
greatest Gothic buildings, and the Museo
dell'Opera, sheltering Duccio's majestic multi-
panelled Maestà.
www.terresiena.it

🔒 19K

ℹ️ Piazza del Campo 56 ☎ 0577/280 551 🕐 Daily 9–7

Duomo

Best places to see, pages 42–43.

Museo dell'Opera del Duomo

This museum occupies part of a half-finished
extension to the cathedral, which would have
made it the largest church in Italy (work was
abandoned following the Black Death in 1348). It
opens with the Gallerie delle Statue, with a tondo
by Donatello in the middle of the room, a *Madonna
and Child* by Jacopo della Quercia and wall statues
by Giovanni Pisano from the cathedral's façade.
Upstairs, in a special room, stands Duccio's
Maestà (1308–11), a magnificent work consisting
of a vast main altarpiece and countless tiny panels.
Other treats are the *Madonna dagli Occhi Grossi*
(Madonna of the Large Eyes) and the view from
the tower.

✉ Piazza del Duomo 8 ☎ 0577/283 048;
www.operaduomo.siena.it ⏰ Mar–May, Sep, Oct daily
9:30–7; Jun–Aug 9:30–8; Nov–Feb 10–5 💰 Expensive

Palazzo Pubblico

The Palazzo Pubblico's medieval outline
dominates the Campo's southern flank. Begun
in 1297, it was designed as civic offices and still
houses various council departments. From its
courtyard an entrance (on the left) leads to the
Torre del Mangia (102m/632ft; 360 steps),
reputedly named after its first bell-ringer, a
wastrel whose nickname – the *Mangiaguadagni*
– meant 'the eater of profits'. The views from
the summit are breathtaking.

A door to the right of the courtyard leads to
the **Museo Civico,** a series of chambers
decorated by Siena's leading medieval and
Renaissance artists. Some of the city's most
famous paintings are here, including Simone
Martini's exquisite *Maestà* (1315–21) and the
series of paintings by Ambrogio Lorenzetti on
Good and Bad Government (1338). Look for the
equestrian portrait of *Guidoriccio da Fogliano*,
opposite the *Maestà*, controversially attributed
to Martini.

Torre del Mangia

✉ Piazza del Campo 1 ☎ 0577/226 230 ⏰ Mid-Mar
to Oct daily 10–7; Nov to mid-Mar 10–4 💰 Expensive
❓ The tower has 360 steps

Museo Civico

✉ Piazza del Campo 1 ☎ Ticketline: 0577/292 614
⏰ Mid-Mar to Oct daily 10–7; Nov to mid-Mar 10–6
💰 Expensive

Piazza del Campo
Best places to see, pages 50–51.

Pinacoteca Nazionale
Siena's Pinacoteca is one of Italy's finest art galleries, its warren of rooms tracing the development of Sienese painting over some 500 years. A lovely and distinct school, the Sienese painters – notably Duccio – drew their early inspiration from Byzantine art, revelling in gold backgrounds, sumptuous tones and stylized Madonnas. Later artists – Pietro Lorenzetti and Simone Martini in particular – moulded these earlier styles to their own purpose, producing beautifully lyrical paintings whose influence was felt as far afield as England and the Netherlands. The gallery then deals with painters such as Sassetta and Giovanni di Paolo, who took stock of Florentine innovations, blending the traditional Sienese motifs with the new wave of Renaissance thinking. Finally the gallery touches on some of Siena's Mannerist stars.

✉ Palazzo Buonsignori, Via San Pietro 29 ☎ 0577/286 143 🕐 Sun, Mon 9–1, Tue–Sat 10–6 💰 Moderate

Sant'Agostino
Begun in 1258, Sant'Agostino's interior was remodelled along baroque lines by Vanvitelli some 500 years later. The church keeps

very irregular hours, but is well worth visiting for a handful of outstanding paintings. Perugino's *Crucifixion* (1506) occupies the second altar of the right (south) aisle. Alongside it, the Cappella Piccolomini contains an *Adoration of the Magi* (1518) by Sodoma and a 14th-century lunette fresco of the *Madonna and Child with Saints* by Ambrogio Lorenzetti. The Cappella Bichi in the south transept has more frescoes and two monochrome medallions by Luca Signorelli.

✉ Prato di Sant'Agostino ☎ None 🕐 Hours vary, consult tourist office
✋ Free

San Domenico

This vast Gothic church, also known as Basilica Cateriniana, is associated with St Catherine of Siena, Italy's joint patron saint (with St Francis). The Cappella delle Volte, right of the entrance, features a contemporary portrait (1414) of the saint, and the Cappella di Santa Caterina (midway down the right aisle) has frescoes of scenes from her life by Sodoma (1526). Her skull is kept in the chapel's altar tabernacle. Left of the chapel is a detached fresco of the *Madonna and Child* by Pietro Lorenzetti, brother of Ambrogio (both probably died in the plague of 1384). The first chapel to the right of the high altar houses Matteo di Giovanni's triptych of the *Madonna and Child with Saints*. Adorning the high altar are a tabernacle and sculpted angels (1475) by Benedetto da Maiano; the second chapel to its left has a *St Barbara and Saints* (Matteo di Giovanni's masterpiece) and *Madonna and Child* by Benvenuto di Giovanni.

✉ Piazza San Domenico ☎ No phone number; www.basilicacateriniana.com
🕐 Mar–Oct daily 7–6:30; Nov–Feb 9–6 ✋ Free

San Francesco

A fire in 1655 left San Francesco stripped of all but a few works of art. Surviving fragments include a *Crucifixion* (1331) by Pietro Lorenzetti (first chapel left of high altar) and two graphic frescoes by Pietro and his brother Ambrogio (third chapel). The sacristy has a fine polyptych by Lippo Vanni of the *Madonna and Child with Four Saints* (1370), and at the end of the right (south) aisle is the 14th-century tomb of the Tolomei. Outside the church is the **Oratorio di San Bernardino,** whose beautifully panelled upper chapel has 14 large frescoes (1496–1518) by Sodoma, Beccafumi and Girolamo del Pacchia.

✉ Piazza San Francesco ☎ Oratorio di San Bernardino: 0577/283 048
🕐 Church: daily 9–12, 3–5. Oratorio di San Bernardino: Mar–Oct daily 10:30–1:30, 3–5:30. Closed Nov–Feb ✋ Church: free. Oratorio: inexpensive

Santa Maria della Scala

For almost 800 years this large building opposite the Duomo served as an orphanage and hospital. Following its recent closure there are plans to turn it into a vast cultural centre. More and more of the medieval complex is being opened to the public, revealing superlative works of art hidden from view for centuries. Chief of these is a vast fresco cycle (1444) by Domenico di Bartolo and Vecchietta, whose perfectly preserved panels decorate what until recently was a large hospital ward. The pictures show the foundation and daily life of the medieval hospital. A smaller stone-vaulted chapel, the Sagrestia Vecchia, is decorated with another fresco cycle by Vecchietta, who sculpted the famous high altar statue of the *Risen Christ* in SS Annunziata, the hospital's former church. In the bowels of the building lies the eerie Oratorio di Santa Caterina della Notte, where St Catherine once passed nocturnal vigils.

www.santamaria.comune.siena.it
✉ Piazza del Duomo 2 ☎ 0577/224 811 🕐 Daily 10:30–6:30 ✋ Moderate
🍴 Shop/café (€)

Santa Maria dei Servi

This outlying church is worth the walk for its works of art and the lovely view of the city from its shady terrace. The first main altar on the right contains the *Madonna di Bordone* (1261) by Coppo di Marcovaldo, a Florentine artist; the last altar on the right features Matteo di Giovanni's *Massacre of the Innocents* (1491). An earlier version of the latter subject by Pietro Lorenzetti occupies the right wall of the second chapel right of the high altar. Other works include *The Adoration of the Shepherds* (1404) by one of Lorenzetti's followers, Taddeo di Bartolo; *Madonna della Misericordia* (1431) by one of Taddeo's pupils, Giovanni di Paolo; and *Madonna del Belvedere* (1363) by Jacopo di Mino.

✉ Piazza Manzoni ☎ None 🕐 Daily 9–12:30, 3–5

✋ Free

a drive around Chianti

Leave Siena (▶ 168–173) to the north, picking up the SR222 towards Castellina in Chianti (21km/13 miles). From Castellina take the SR429 east to Radda in Chianti (10km/6 miles). Two kilometres (1.2 miles) east of Radda at Villa there is an optional scenic circuit to the north (15km/9 miles), via Volpaia. Return to the main road at Villa.

The SR222 is one of the more scenic roads in Chianti, but like many in the region it is fairly twisting, so distances are often a good deal longer than they appear on the map. Both Castellina and Radda are major wine producers, and both have pretty central cores, but their outskirts have been tarnished by new building. Volpaia has an evocative 16th-century castle and several watchtowers.

From Radda head east to Badia a Coltibuono (6km/4 miles) and then drive south on the SP408 to Gaiole in Chianti (5km/3 miles). South of the village (3km/

2 miles), turn left and follow a lovely minor road past Castagnoli, Linari and San Gusmé (20km/12 miles). Turn right on the SS484 to Castello di Brolio (8km/5 miles).

Badia is part of an abbey complex owned by one of Chianti's leading producers. You can eat in the restaurant here (see below for details) or buy wine, honey and virgin olive oil from the estate shop. Gaiole is an unexceptional village, but the Castello di Brolio is more appealing. One of Chianti's oldest vineyards, it has been owned by the Ricasoli family since 1141. Wine can be bought here also, and there are occasional organized tours of the winery.

From Brolio return to Siena (26km/16 miles) on the SP408 via San Giovanni.

Distance 110km (68 miles) depending on optional detours
Time Allow a day
Start/end point Siena ✚ 19K
Lunch Restaurant (€€) ✉ Badia a Coltibuono ☎ 0577/749 424; www.coltibuono.com ◷ May–Oct daily 12–10:30; mid-Mar to Apr, Nov to mid-Jan Tue–Sun 12–10:30. Closed mid-Jan to mid-Mar

VOLTERRA

Volterra commands wide views across eerie grey-brown hills, many riddled with the deposits of alum and alabaster that have long been the region's economic mainstay. Learn more in the Alabaster Museum (Museo Storico dell'Alabastro). The Piazza dei Priori is home to the Palazzo dei Priori (1208–57), known for Orcagna's painting of the *Annunciation* (1383) in the first-floor Sala del Consiglio. Also here is the Torre del Porcellino (Piglet's Tower), named after the carved boar to the right of the top window, and the former Bishops' Palace, part of which is taken up with the **Museo d'Arte Sacra.**

Backing on to Piazza dei Priori is the Piazza del Duomo, site of a Baptistery (closed for restoration) and the Duomo, with Mino da Fiesole's high altar tabernacle and sculpted angels (1471) and a painted background by Benozzo Gozzoli to two terracotta figures by Zaccaria da Voltera (north aisle). North is the **Pinacoteca-Museo Civico,** renowned for Rosso Fiorentino's *Descent from the Cross* (1521), and earlier Sienese and Florentine paintings. Look for the *balze*, Volterra's famous eroded cliffs; the Roman theatre and other sights in the town's Archaeological Zone (to the north); and the wealth of Etruscan objects in the **Museo Etrusco Guarnacci.**

✚ 16J

ℹ️ Piazza dei Priori 20 ☎ 0588/87 257; www.volterratur.it

Museo d'Arte Sacra

✉️ Via Roma 13 ☎ 0588/86 290 🕐 Mid-Mar to mid-Oct daily 9–1, 3–6; mid-Oct to mid-Mar 9–1 💰 Expensive

Museo Etrusco Guarnacci

✉️ Via Don Minzoni 15 ☎ 0588/86 347 🕐 Mid-Mar to Oct daily 9–7; Nov to mid-Mar 9–1:45 💰 Expensive. Joint ticket with Pinacoteca

Pinacoteca-Museo Civico

✉️ Via dei Sarti 1 ☎ 0588/87 580 🕐 Mid-Mar to Oct daily 9–7; Nov to mid-Mar 8:30–1:45 💰 Expensive. Joint ticket with Museo Etrusco Guarnacci

HOTELS

AREZZO
Badia di Pomaio (€–€€)

Four kilometres (2.5 miles) outside the city, with wonderful views across the Tuscan countryside, this 17th-century monastery is a wonderfully tranquil place to stay. There's an excellent restaurant.

✉ Localita Pomaio 4 ☎ 0575/371 407; www.badiadipomaio.it

CORTONA
Hotel San Michele (€€)

A glorious Renaissance *palazzo* whose elegance was retained following its conversion into a four-star hotel. There's plenty of old-world grandeur, and some antique-filled period rooms. Central location.

✉ Via Guelfa 15 ☎ 0575/604 348; www.hotelsanmichele.net

MONTALCINO
Il Giglio (€–€€)

An inn for over a century, this moderately elegant hotel in central Montalcino has been improved by renovation work. Many of the 12 rooms (plus 6 in the annexe) enjoy views over the *crete* and Orcia valley.

✉ Via Soccorso Saloni 5 ☎ 0577/846 577; www.gigliohotel.com

MONTEPULCIANO
Duomo (€)

This is the best all-round mid-priced hotel in town. Located just a few steps up the street from the cathedral square. Be sure to reserve ahead.

✉ Via San Donato 14 ☎ 0578/757 473; www.albergoduomo.it

PIENZA
Il Chiostro di Pienza Relais (€€–€€€)

This beautifully converted central hotel has 37 tasteful rooms which form part of a former monastery and are entered from an elegant courtyard *(chiostro)*.

✉ Corso Il Rossellino 26 ☎ 0578/748 400; www.relaisilchiostrodipienza.com

SAN GIMIGNANO
La Cisterna (€–€€)
There is little to choose between San Gimignano's major central hotels: La Cisterna has pleasant rooms and a perfect position at the heart of everything. Try to get a room with country or piazza views.

✉ Piazza della Cisterna 24 ☎ 0577/940 328; www.hotelcisterna.it

Leon Bianco (€–€€)
An elegant hotel in a medieval town house, more intimate than La Cisterna, with 24 rooms.

✉ Piazza della Cisterna 13 ☎ 0577/941 294; www.leonbianco.com

SIENA
Antica Torre (€)
Eight tasteful, mid-sized rooms in a converted medieval tower make this the most intimate and stylish mid-price option in the city. Reserve ahead.

✉ Via Fiera Vecchia 7 ☎ 0577/222 255; www.anticatorresiena.it

Palazzo Ravizza (€€)
A peaceful hotel in a peripheral but charming part of the city. A pension since 1929, it is in an 18th-century *palazzo* with rooms of varying quality and charm. Reservations essential.

✉ Pian dei Mantellini 34 ☎ 0577/280 462; www.palazzoravizza.it

VOLTERRA
Etruria (€)
A reasonably priced three-star hotel on the main street in central Volterra.

✉ Via Matteotti 32 ☎ 0588/87 377; www.albergoetruria.it

RESTAURANTS

AREZZO
Antica Osteria L'Agania (€)
An authentic and intimate Tuscan trattoria, with a good choice of local dishes based on the region's traditional cooking: things like

polenta, *panzanella* (Tuscan salad), *minestrone*, *ribollita* and *coniglio alla porchetta* (rabbit stew). Just south of Piazza Grande.
✉ Via Mazzini 10 ☎ 0575/295 381; www.agania.com 🕐 Closed Mon and part of Jun

La Lancia d'Oro (€€)

First choice for a treat, if only for the Piazza Grande setting. Well-executed local specialties such as filling *zuppa di farro* (soup made with a type of grain grown locally) and a variety of tender grilled meats. Fresh fish is sometimes available on Fridays.
✉ Piazza Grande 18, Logge Vasari ☎ 0575/21 033 🕐 Closed Sun evening, Mon and part of Nov

Il Saraceno (€)

A stone's throw from L'Agania and offering a similarly authentic trattoria experience (though with three times as many seats). The food is perhaps a touch better, with superb desserts (try the *marscarpone al caffè*), mouthwatering *ribollita*, succulent *zuppa di porcini* and decadent *ravioli al tartufo*. Serves gluten-free dishes.
✉ Via Mazzini 6B ☎ 0575/27 644; www.ilsaraceno.com 🕐 Closed Wed, Sun pm and for a period in Jul or Aug

CASTELLINA IN CHIANTI
L'Albergaccio (€€)

Any tour of Chianti will probably require a stop for lunch: Castellina has two good options. This is marginally the better and more expensive of the two. The dining room is pretty and in good weather you can eat outdoors. The food is classic Tuscan, with the bonus of homemade pastas.
✉ Via Fiorentina 63 ☎ 0577/741 042 🕐 Closed Sun evening, Wed lunch and early Jan

COLLE DI VAL D'ELSA
L'Antica Trattoria (€€€)

Despite its less than perfect position – in the lower and newer part of Colle on a square bustling with cars and buses – the chances are you will have one of your better Tuscan meals in this superb Michelin-starred restaurant. As well as much-loved staples such as *zuppa di legumi* (soup made with lentils, beans, chickpeas and barley) and *l'anatra all uva* (duck with grapes), the owner regularly experiments with new and invariably successful dishes.

✉ Piazza Arnolfo 23 ☎ 0577/923 747 ◷ Closed Tue, 25 Dec–6 Jan

Arnolfo (€€€)

If you want to blow the budget on a long lunch then Arnolfo takes some beating. The service is impeccable and the dishes, using local ingredients, are innovative.

✉ Via XX Settembre 50 ☎ 0577/920 549; www.arnolfo.com ◷ Thu–Mon 12–2:30, 7–9:30. Closed Tue, Wed and mid-Jan to early Mar

CORTONA
Il Preludio (€€)

Housed in part of a medieval *palazzo* at the heart of Cortona, this pleasant restaurant offers food in a classic Tuscan style, enlivened with occasional touches of invention. Pastas and *antipasti* are all homemade, the *risotti*, in particular, being especially good.

✉ Via Guelfa 11 ☎ 0575/630 104; www.ilpreludio.net ◷ Closed Mon Nov–Easter

MONTALCINO
Il Moro (€)

The first choice for a straightforward meal in modern trattoria surroundings at prices that will not break the bank.

✉ Via Mazzini 44 ☎ 0577/849 384 ◷ Closed Thu

Taverna Grappola Blu (€–€€)

Just two pleasant, small stone-walled rooms and often superb and innovative food. Pastas are especially interesting and unusual. The restaurant is popular, so be sure to reserve a table. Service can be slow at busy times.

✉ Via Scale di Moglio 1, signed off Via Mazzini ☎ 0577/847 150
◷ Closed Fri

MONTEPULCIANO
Caffè Poliziano (€–€€)
Montepulciano's nicest café has a lovely art nouveau interior. In addition, there is a separate restaurant for full meals.

✉ Via di Voltaia nel Corso 27–29 ☎ 0578/758 615 ⓒ Restaurant closed Wed

Diva (€)
Diva is something of an institution, though it is no longer quite the old-world and undiscovered trattoria it once was. The menu is limited – little more than grilled meats for the main course – but all is perfectly cooked. It's popular and inexpensive, so be sure to arrive early to secure a table. If upstairs is full, there is more room downstairs. Situated in the lower part of town, just inside the walls.

✉ Via Gracciano nel Corso 92 ☎ 0578/716 951 ⓒ Closed Tue and three weeks in Jul

MONTERIGGIONI
Ristorante Il Piccolo Castello (€–€€)
In the heart of a delightful walled village, this rustic Tuscan dining room is a pretty place to enjoy a menu of local dishes. In winter you can try dishes flavoured with the prized white truffle.

✉ Via 1 Maggio 1 ☎ 0577/304 370; www.ristoranteilpiccolocastello.com ⓒ Closed Tue in low season

PIENZA
Dal Falco (€–€€)
A welcoming, family-run trattoria just outside the walls, with several snug dining rooms and plenty of Tuscan specialties. Try the superb *gnocchi* or the *pecorino alla griglia* (sheep's cheese – a Pienzan delicacy – wrapped in ham and grilled).

✉ Piazza Dante Alighieri 7 ☎ 0578/748 551; www.ristorantedalfalco.it ⓒ Closed Fri

Latte di Luna (€–€€)
A friendly and traditional Pienzan restaurant in an evocative little corner on the eastern end of Pienza's short main street. It has a

small terrace for al fresco eating in summer, and an ancient well is incorporated into the medieval interior.

✉ Piazza San Carlo 2–4 ☎ 0578/748 606 🕐 Closed Tue

SAN GIMIGNANO
Ristorante Dorandò (€€€)

The town's most expensive and most ambitious restaurant prides itself on creating 'historic' dishes of Renaissance and Etruscan vintage. This may sound dubious, but the results are usually excellent. The restaurant's elegant ambience is offset by deliberately rustic touches.

✉ Vicolo dell'Oro 2, off Piazza della Cisterna ☎ 0577/941 862; www.ristorantedorando.it 🕐 Closed Mon in low season and Dec, Jan

Le Vecchie Mura (€–€€)

Attractively set in a vaulted former stable, built within the old town walls. Owned by the same family since it opened in the 1980s, the restaurant had a revamp in 2008, but the menu still concentrates on excellent Tuscan dishes.

✉ Via Piandornella 15 ☎ 0577/940 270; www.vecchiemura.it 🕐 Closed Tue

SIENA
Antica Osteria da Divo (€€–€€€)

There are some remarkable subterranean medieval dining rooms here and an upstairs dining area that is almost as atmospheric. The food is also more than acceptable. Located a little way north of the Duomo.

✉ Via Franciosa 29 ☎ 0577/286 054; www.osteriadadivo.it 🕐 Closed Sun in winter

Il Campo (€€€)

It's not every day you have the chance to dine out in one of Europe's loveliest squares. So if you want to treat yourself, this is the restaurant to go for. Avoid the four tourist menus and go for the traditional *à la carte* options instead.

✉ Piazza del Campo 50 ☎ 0577/280 725; www.ristoranteilcampo.com
🕐 Closed Tue and four weeks in Jan and Feb

Nello (€€)

If Osteria Le Logge (almost opposite) is closed or full, or you wish to spend a little less, this easygoing restaurant makes an ideal alternative. You see the day's pasta being made and laid out as you enter – always a good sign – and the food when it arrives lives up to first impressions. A nice single medieval dining room, plus a few tables outside in summer.

✉ Via del Porrione 28–30 ☎ 0577/289 043 ⊘ Closed Sun and Jan

Osteria del Fico Mezzo (€–€€)

A tremendous addition to Siena's rather predictable crop of restaurants: innovative food; a tasteful single-room dining area (cool and pastel-painted); and good value, especially at lunchtime, when you can choose between a handful of set-price mini menus.

✉ Via dei Termini 71 ☎ 0577/222 384; www.ficomezzo.net ⊘ Closed Sun and mid-Jul to mid-Aug

Osteria Le Logge (€€)

This is Siena's prettiest restaurant, thanks to its lovely cabinet-lined interior – the building was formerly an old pharmacy. The food, however, once considered outstanding, has slipped. Located just a few steps east of the Campo. Be sure to reserve ahead.

✉ Via del Porrione 33 ☎ 0577/48 013; www.giannibrunelli.it ⊘ Closed Sun and Jan

Sotto le Fonti (€–€€)

This simple *osteria* has an excellent reputation for traditional Tuscan food. The menu is seasonal and the desserts are always made in-house. It's off the main tourist routes, so get directions from your hotel.

✉ Via Esterna Fontebranda 114, Santa Caterina ☎ 0577 226 446; www.sottolefonti.it ⊘ Tue–Sat 12:20–3, 8–11

La Torre (€€)

This single-room trattoria, no longer the undiscovered gem it once was, plays slightly on its old-world authenticity, and prices have risen as a result. However, it remains popular, so arrive early or reserve in person to be sure of a table. There's rarely any menu, so follow the advice of the waiter. The off-Campo location is convenient.

✉ Via Salicotto 7 ☎ 0577/287 548 🕓 Closed Thu

VOLTERRA
Da Badò (€–€€)
An excellent restaurant with a high reputation for its well-cooked Volterran specialties.

✉ Borgo San Lazzaro 9, just east of Volterra on the SS68 road ☎ 0588/86 477; www.trattoriadabado.com 🕓 Closed Wed and Jul

Trattoria del Sacco Fiorentino (€–€€)
This restaurant offers classic Tuscan cooking with a slight innovatory twist. Prices in the small adjoining *enoteca* (wine bar) area are lower.

✉ Piazza XX Settembre 18 ☎ 0588/88 537 🕓 Closed Wed and Jan

SHOPPING

MARKETS
Montalcino
Old-fashioned market full of locals in the shadow of the town's fairy-tale fortress.

✉ Piazzale Fortezza 🕓 Fri 7–1

Montepulciano
A big bustling market by the old walls in the lower town.

✉ Porta al Prato 🕓 Thu am

Pienza
A tiny but interesting market held just outside the old walls of the village.

✉ Viale Mencatelli 🕓 Fri am

San Gimignano
An intimate little market in the village's main square.

✉ Piazza del Duomo 🕓 Thu and Sat 7–1

Siena

The general market in La Lizza is a huge affair. Piazza del Mercato is where many Sienese shop for everyday fruit and vegetables.

✉ La Lizza, Viale Cesare Maccari ⏰ Wed am

✉ Piazza del Mercato ⏰ Mon–Sat 7–1

Volterra

A little market in one of the town's central main squares.

✉ Piazza dei Priori ⏰ Sat 7:30–1:30

ENTERTAINMENT

CLASSICAL MUSIC

Accademia Musicale Chigiana

Tuscany in the summer offers a wealth of small-town cultural festivals. One of the most prestigious belongs to Siena, where the *Settimana Musicale Senese* in July sees a week of performances by the acclaimed Accademia Musicale Chigiana.

✉ Via di Città 89, Siena ☎ 0577/22 091; www.chigiana.it ⏰ Jul–early Aug

Cantiere Internazionale d'Arte

Montepulciano's Cantiere Internazionale d'Arte (July–August) concentrates on new or more avant-garde works by composers, dramatists and choreographers. If you are unable to attend these larger festivals, enquire at tourist offices or keep your eyes open for posters advertising small church or other year-round recitals.

✉ Via Fiorenzuola 5, Montepulciano ☎ 0578/757 089; www.fondazionecantiere.it ⏰ Jul–Aug

San Gimignano

Less exalted than the Festival Pucciniano or the *Settimana Musicale Senese*, but more varied and intimate, is the San Gimignano festival (in July), which has been held in the village since the 1920s. It offers music, film and theatrical presentations, usually culminating in two gala opera performances outdoors in the Piazza del Duomo. As with many of the festivals, reserve early (ideally before starting your holiday) to avoid disappointment.

✉ Piazza del Duomo 1 ☎ 0577/940 008; www.sangimignano.com ⏰ Jul

Index

Acknowledgements

The Automobile Association would like to thank the following photographers, companies and picture libraries for their assistance in the preparation of this book.

Abbreviations for the picture credits are as follows: - (t) top; (b) bottom; (l) left; (r) right; (c) centre; (AA) AA World Travel Library.

6/7 Tuscan countryside AA/K Paterson; **8/9** Olives AA/ K Paterson; **10bl** via di San Salvatore AA/S McBride; **10/11t** Chianti countryside AA/K Paterson; **10c** Piazza della Signoria AA/S McBride; **10br** Palazzo Vecchio AA/C Sawyer; **11bl** Piazza del Campo AA/T Harris; **12bl** Como AA/M Jourdan; **12/13t** Tuscan dish AA/T Harris; **12c** Beans AA/T Souter; **12br** Cheeses AA/S McBride;

13cl Honey AA/K Paterson; **13bl** Cantucci AA/T Harris; **14/15** Wine tasting AA/T Harris; **15** Wine AA/T Harris; **16bl** Duomo AA/S McBride; **16br** David AA/S McBride; **16/17** Ice cream AA/S McBride; **17bl** Piazza del Campo AA/C Sawyer; **18** Ponte Vecchio AA/C Sawyer; **19tl** Florence AA/B Smith; **19tr** Boboli gardens AA/S McBride; **19c** Uffizi AA/S McBride; **19b** San Gimignano AA/S McBride; **20/21** Piazza della Signoria AA/S McBride; **24bl** Festival AA/T Harris; **26** Station AA/T Harris; **27br** Ferry AA/T Harris; **31cr** Telephone box AA/M Jourdan; **34/35** Siena AA/S McBride; **36/37** Medici Chapel AA/T Harris; **38/9t** Collegiata AA/R Ireland; **38/39b** Fresco AA/C Sawyer; **40** David AA/S McBride; **41tl** David AA/K Paterson; **42/43** Duomo AA/T Harris; **44tl** Uffizi AA/S McBride; **44bl** Uffizi AA; **45** Uffizi AA/S McBride; **46tr** Bargello AA/S McBride; **46b** Courtyard AA/S McBride; **47tr** Lion AA/S McBride; **48/49t** Museo di San Marco AA/C Sawyer; **48c** San Marco AA/S McBride; **49b** Fresco AA/S McBride; **50/51** Piazza del Campo AA/J Edmanson; **50bl** Siena AA/T Souter; **52** Santa Croce AA/S McBride; **53tr** Galileo's Tomb AA/S McBride; **53c** Santa Croce AA/S McBride; **54c** Duomo and Baptistery AA/T Harris; **54/55** Campanile AA/T Souter; **56/57** San Gimignano AA/S McBride; **58** Montalcino AA/C Sawyer; **60** Ospedale degli Innocenti AA/C Sawyer; **62/63** Piazzale Michelangelo, Chad Ehlers/Alamy; **65** San Lorenzo Market, Florence AA/T Harris; **66/67** San Gimignano AA/K Paterson; **68/9t** Ice cream AA/A Mockford & N Bonetti; **69br** Parco di Pinocchio AA/K Paterson; **70bl** Fiesole AA/T Harris; **72/73** Santa Maria Novella AA/S McBride; **74/75** San Lorenzo AA/T Harris; **77bl** Ponte Vecchio AA/C Sawyer; **78/79** Battistero AA/C Sawyer; **79br** Battistero AA/S McBride; **80cr** Campanile AA/S McBride; **81** Campanile AA/S McBride; **82/83** Santa Maria del Carmine AA/S McBride; **84/85t** Casa Buonarroti AA/T Harris; **85b** Duomo AA/S McBride; **86** Duomo AA/K Paterson; **87tr** Duomo AA/S McBride; **88bl** Fountain AA/S McBride; **88/89t** Museo della Casa Fiorentina Antica AA/C Sawyer; **90tr** Museo Bardini AA/C Sawyer; **90/91b** Museo de Firenze com'era AA/J Edmanson; **92b** San Miniato al Monte AA/C Sawyer; **94/95** Museo dell'Opera del Duomo AA/S McBride; **95tr** Museo dell'Opera del Duomo AA/S McBride; **96/97** Museo di Storia della Scienza AA/C Sawyer; **98/99t** Orsanmichele AA/C Sawyer; **98bl** Orsanmichele AA/C Sawyer; **99cl** Orsanmichele AA/T Harris; **100bl** Palazzo Medici-Riccardi AA/C Sawyer; **100/101b** Frescoes AA/C Sawyer; **101tl** Gardens AA/B Smith; **102/103t** Palazzo Pitti AA/S McBride; **102/103b** Palazzo Pitti AA/S McBride; **104tl** Palazzo Pitti AA/S McBride; **104/105** Palazzo Vecchio AA/J Edmanson; **106** Piazza della Signoria AA/C Sawyer; **107tr** Lions AA/C Sawyer; **108/109** Ponte Vecchio AA/S McBride; **110/111t** Santissima Annunziata AA/C Sawyer; **112tr** San Lorenzo AA/T Harris; **113b** San Lorenzo AA/B Smith; **115** Santa Maria Novella AA/S McBride; **116** Santa Maria Novella AA/T Harris; **117t** Cloister AA/S McBride; **118tr** San Miniato al Monte AA/ C Sawyer; **119tr** Pulpit AA/B Smith; **119bl** Piazza di Santa Trinità AA/T Harris; **120t** Fresco AA/S McBride; **133tl** Altagnana AA/C Sawyer; **134tr** Near Carrara AA/C Sawyer; **135tr** Pulpit AA/T Harris; **135b** Barga AA/T Harris; **136tr** Quarries AA/K Paterson; **137b** Villa Poggio a Caiano, near Empoli AA/K Paterson; **138c** Duomo AA/K Paterson; **139** Castelnuovo di Garfagnana AA/K Paterson; **140b** Lucca AA/K Paterson; **140/141t** Lucca AA/C Sawyer; **142/143t** San Frediano AA/C Sawyer; **142/143c** San Frediano AA/C Sawyer; **143bl** San Michele AA/K Paterson; **144/145t** Montecatini Terme AA/K Paterson; **145bl** Duomo AA/C Sawyer; **146/147b** Battistero AA/C Sawyer; **147c** Prato AA/C Sawyer; **148b** Viareggio AA/T Harris; **153b** San Quirico d'Orcia AA/K Paterson; **154t** Abbazia di Monte Oliveto Maggiore AA/T Harris; **155tr** Arezzo AA/C Sawyer; **156/157t** Piazza della Repubblica AA/T Harris; **156cl** Cortona AA/T Harris; **156/157b** Montalcino AA/S McBride; **158/159b** San Biaggio AA/S McBride; **161** Pienza AA/S McBride; **162t** San Gimignano AA/K Paterson; **164tl** Piazza della Cisterna AA/S McBride; **164/165** Piazza della Cisterna AA/S McBride; **165tr** Sant'Agostino AA/S McBride; **167b** San Quirico d'Orcia AA/K Paterson; **168/169** Duomo AA/S McBride; **170** Sant'Agostino AA/T Harris; **171** Basilica AA/T Harris; **173b** Santa Maria dei Servi AA/S McBride; **174br** Vines AA/K Paterson; **175t** Chianti farmhouse AA/J Edmanson; **176tr** Volterra AA/R Ireland

Every effort has been made to trace the copyright holders, and we apologise in advance for any accidental errors. We would be happy to apply the corrections in the following edition of this publication.

Sight locator index

This index relates to the maps on the covers. We have given map references to the main sights in the book. Grid references in italics indicate sights featured on the town plan. Some sights within towns may not be plotted on the maps.